Read and Respond Journal

GRADE 5

Copyright © by Houghton Mifflin Harcourt Publishing Company

All rights reserved. No part of this work may be reproduced or transmitted in any form or by any means, electronic or mechanical, including photocopying or recording, or by any information storage or retrieval system, without the prior written permission of the copyright owner unless such copying is expressly permitted by federal copyright law.

Permission is hereby granted to individuals using the corresponding student's textbook or kit as the major vehicle for regular classroom instruction to photocopy entire pages from this publication in classroom quantities for instructional use and not for resale. Requests for information on other matters regarding duplication of this work should be submitted through our Permissions website at https://customercare.hmhco.com/contactus/Permissions.html or mailed to Houghton Mifflin Harcourt Publishing Company, Attn: Intellectual Property Licensing, 9400 Southpark Center Loop, Orlando, Florida 32819-8647.

Printed in the U.S.A.

ISBN 978-0-358-25496-6

11 2023

4500879846   r6.23

If you have received these materials as examination copies free of charge, Houghton Mifflin Harcourt Publishing Company retains title to the materials and they may not be resold. Resale of examination copies is strictly prohibited.

Possession of this publication in print format does not entitle users to convert this publication, or any portion of it, into electronic format.

Contents

MODULE 1
- Women of the American Revolution 2
- Making a Magazine 10
- Making a Movie 18

MODULE 2
- A Trip to a Cave 26
- The Twin Twins 34
- Counting Birds 42

MODULE 3
- An Ocean Learner 50
- Sojourner Truth: Speaker for Equal Rights 58
- No Tea for Me! 66

MODULE 4
- Bison Come Back to the Plains 74
- Nero Hawley's Dream 82
- Horse Rider 90

MODULE 5
- The Rescue Helicopter Team 98
- Oil Spill in Alaska 106
- The Long Flight 114

MODULE 6
- On the Beckwourth Trail 122
- The Carpenter and the Drummer Boy 130
- Tomás Decides 138

MODULE 7
- The Story of Bunker's Cove 146
- The Cattle Drive 154
- It Takes Teamwork 162

MODULE 8
- Stonehenge: A Riddle 170
- In the Year 2525 178
- Orphan Boy and the Elk Dogs 186

MODULE 9
- The All-Wrong All-Stars 194
- Protector of the Wilderness 202
- Off to Oregon 210

MODULE 10
- Nothing Ever Happens in the Country 218
- Will the American Chestnut Survive? 226
- The Many Faces of Rolling Hills 234

MODULE 1 WEEK 1

Women of the American Revolution

by Mia Lewis

Men did most of the fighting against the British. Women, young and old, played a part, too. They did many things to help win the war.

Women stopped buying British goods. They made their own cloth. They kept their family farms running when the men were off fighting.

Women gave food and shelter to the troops. They gave the men advice and support. Some women worked as spies. A few even took up arms.

READ & RESPOND

Author's Purpose

Look at the title. Do you think this text is meant to inform or entertain? Explain.

_____
_____
_____

Lydia Darragh lived in Philadelphia. The British took control of the city in 1777. Many Patriots fled, but Lydia and her family stayed behind.

General Howe led the British troops. He and his men set up a meeting using the Darraghs' dining room. Lydia and her family were told to go to sleep. Lydia stayed awake, however. She listened at the keyhole and heard the British talk. They were planning a surprise attack on the Patriots!

READ & RESPOND

Central Idea

What details show that Lydia Darragh's story belongs in this text?

___
___
___

Lydia said she needed flour. The British gave her a pass to leave the city. She dropped off her flour sack at the mill and kept walking. She walked until she met her friend Thomas Craig.

Craig was in the colonial army. Lydia told him what she had heard. Then she picked up her flour and went home. Craig passed on the warning.

The Americans were ready for their foes when the British arrived. Howe had to retreat without firing a shot. Lydia had saved the day.

READ & RESPOND

Central Idea

How did Lydia Darragh help the American Revolution?

_____
_____
_____

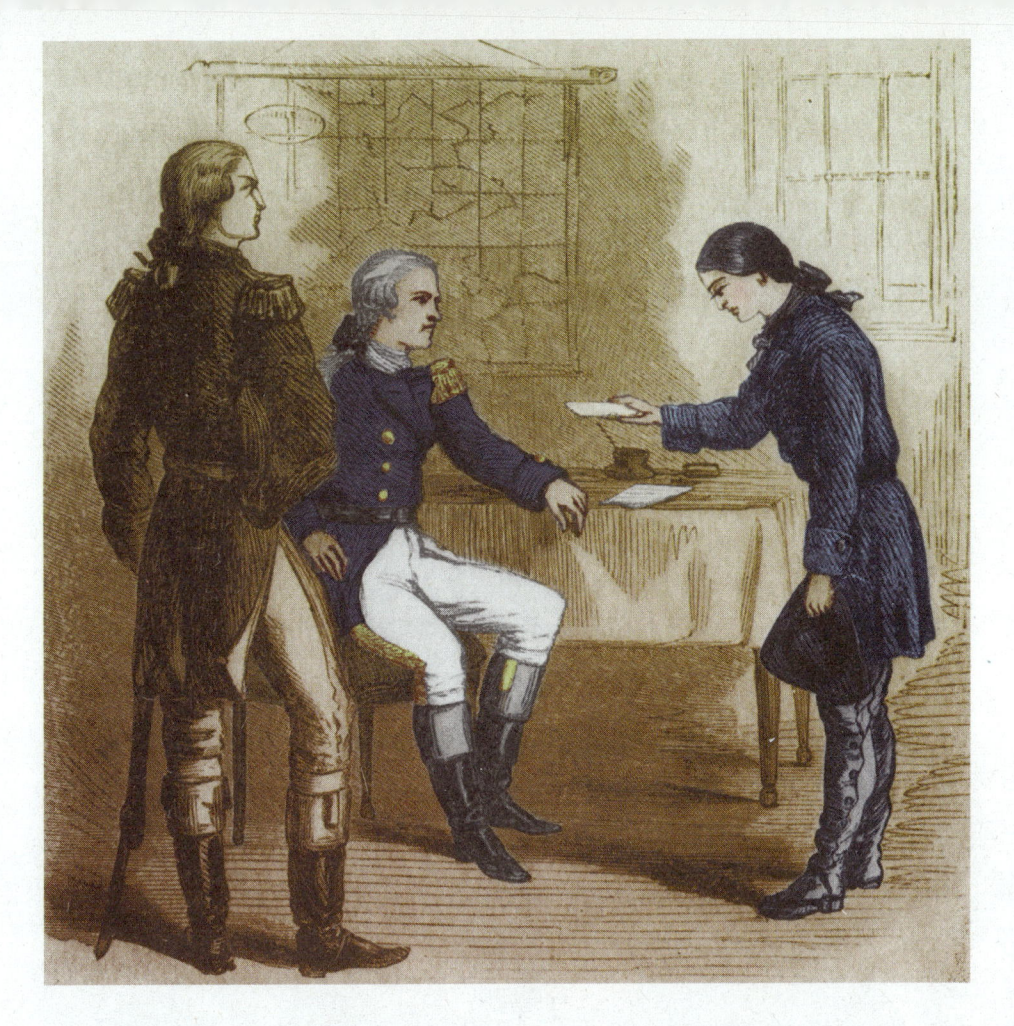

Deborah Sampson wanted to fight the British. Women could not join the army, so her strategy was to go to war as a man! She signed up as "Robert Shurtleff." She dressed as a man, and she fought as a man. No one in the army knew her secret.

Deborah was in several battles. She was wounded more than once. She let the army doctor treat a deep cut on her head. She hid her other wounds, afraid that doctors would find out she was a woman.

READ & RESPOND

Author's Purpose

Why do you think the author included the story of Deborah Sampson in this text?

_____
_____
_____

One day Deborah got really sick. She had a high fever. A doctor treated her and found out her secret. He kept quiet about it. He treated her until she was well again.

"Robert Shurtleff" got an honorable discharge from the army. Deborah put her own clothes back on and went home. She later married and had three children. Deborah asked for a pension for her service. She was the first woman to get an army pension.

> **READ & RESPOND**
>
> Central Idea
>
> **Why is Deborah Sampson considered an important person of the American Revolution?**
>
> _____
>
> _____

Abigail Adams was the wife of John Adams. John was an important Founding Father. He went to France to speak for America. He was our first vice president and our second president.

John Adams was a hero. He helped bring about a revolution in America. Abigail was a hero, too! She stood up for the rights of women. She gave her husband advice. He always listened to her, and he said that Abigail was one of his best advisers.

READ & RESPOND

Author's Purpose

Why does the author include details about John Adams?

_____

_____

_____

Sometimes John Adams was away from home. So Abigail and John wrote letters. They were friendly letters and weren't too formal. They included news and advice. Abigail and John wrote many letters to each other over the years.

One letter from Abigail to John is famous. John was away for a long time, working with the men in Congress. He was planning for the future of the United States. Abigail sent him a letter. It said, "Remember the ladies!"

READ & RESPOND

Central Idea and Author's Purpose

Why do you think the text ends with the quote by Abigail Adams, "Remember the ladies!"

_____
_____

Reread and Respond

1 **What is this text mainly about? How can you tell?**

_____
_____
_____

> **Hint**
> Look for clues on every page.

2 **Was Deborah Sampson a brave soldier?**

_____
_____
_____

> **Hint**
> For clues, see page 5.

3 **How did Abigail Adams help her country?**

_____
_____
_____

> **Hint**
> For clues, see pages 7 and 8.

4 **In general, how would you describe Patriot women?**

_____
_____
_____

MODULE 1 WEEK 2

Making a Magazine

by Dolores Vasquez

What does it take to make a magazine? Our class was getting ready to find out. We had decided to plan and publish our own magazine.

First, we would learn everything that's required to make a magazine. We'd need to choose story ideas. Then we'd do research and gather facts. We'd write stories and take photographs to go with them.

To get started, we looked at other magazines for ideas. We read the stories. We studied the pictures. We began to discuss plans for our own magazine. What sort of articles should be in the magazine? How should it look?

READ & RESPOND

Text Structure

What transition words give clues about how this text will be structured?

_____
_____
_____

10

Learning from an Expert

"Students," said Mr. Gomez, "I'd like to introduce the best magazine writer in the nation. This is Annie Smith. She travels around the world writing about exciting events. Still, when she first started work, she was closer to home."

Annie told us about her first job. She worked at a magazine in the small town where she grew up. She wrote about interesting people who lived there. Her favorite story was about an old man who ran a bakery. People came from far away to buy his cakes, but they did not know his background. He had once worked as a chef at the White House!

Annie's story about the old man won a prize. That really helped her career take off.

READ & RESPOND

Monitor and Clarify

How does the picture help you understand how Annie is teaching the class?

_____
_____
_____

Planning Stories

Annie gave us many insights into what makes a good magazine story. Now it was time for us to come up with our own story ideas. We decided to follow Annie's formula. We'd interview interesting people in our own neighborhood.

We talked about people who lived and worked nearby. Everyone suggested ideas. Then we chose our favorites. We picked three people to interview.

The class split up into three teams of writers. Each would interview one person and write a story.

READ & RESPOND

Text Structure

How is this part of the text structured? What words in the text help you to know?

_____
_____
_____

My team had come up with a great idea for the magazine. Although we lived in the city, we would write about activities that usually take place in the country.

Shana knew a family who lived near the park. They kept bees. Paul had an uncle who raised chickens.

"Nobody is interested in chickens," said Shana.

"Any subject can be interesting if the writer makes it interesting," said Mr. Gomez. Then he reminded us about the community garden that many of us passed each day on the way to school. How could we find out who had started it? What did people grow there?

"That's a great idea, Mr. G," I said.

READ & RESPOND

Monitor and Clarify

Do you understand what the team is going to write about? What can you do to help you understand?

_____

_____

Conducting an Interview

My team went to the community garden. We asked around and found that it was started by a woman named Laura Antonio. We searched her out. She told us that the garden used to be an empty lot. Now twenty different families grew food there. Laura grew enough tomatoes to make ten gallons of tomato sauce each summer!

We asked Laura about her background. How did she learn how to grow things? Laura explained that she grew up on a farm in Italy. When she moved to the United States, she missed growing things. She decided to start the community garden. She helped other city families grow vegetables there, too.

READ & RESPOND

Text Structure

What clues on this page show that this section of the text will focus on interviews?

_____
_____
_____

Putting It All Together

The interview with Laura gave us great insights into how a community garden works. We learned why gardens are great for the community.

There was still more work to do. We did research in the library and on the Internet. We learned more facts about community gardens to add to our story. Then we wrote the story. We checked to make sure all the information was correct. Finally, we reread the story and made a few changes to improve it.

We had a lot of photographs, and we couldn't decide which ones to use. So, we showed them to another team. Together, we worked out which ones were best.

READ & RESPOND

Monitor and Clarify

Do you understand why this section is called "Putting It All Together"? What clues in the text help you understand?

_____
_____

Publishing the Magazine

At last, we had all finished our stories. Nobody has ever worked so hard! We were ready to put our words and photographs together on the computer. When we were finished, we printed out one copy of the new magazine. We checked it to make sure there were no mistakes. There were mistakes! We fixed them. Then we printed out lots of copies for our friends, families, and other students at school.

We had published our first magazine! We learned a lot and had fun, too. Maybe some of us will be famous magazine writers some day!

READ & RESPOND

Text Structure

Look at the heading on this page. Why do you think the author chose to use headings for this text?

_____
_____

Reread and Respond

1 How does the class get started to learn what is required to make a magazine?

_____
_____
_____

Hint
For clues, see page 10.

2 What insights about community gardens might Laura give that wouldn't be found in books?

_____
_____
_____

Hint
For clues, see pages 14 and 15.

3 Why does the team do more research after they have interviewed Laura?

_____
_____
_____

Hint
For clues, see page 15.

4 On page 16, the narrator says, "There were mistakes!" Is the statement a fact or an opinion? Explain.

_____
_____
_____

Hint
Think about the differences between facts and opinions.

Making a Movie

by Mia Lewis

All the members of the video club were in the film studio of Westlake School. It was their first meeting since the club decided to launch a new project.

"We are going to make our own movie," said Sally.

"We'll base it on a story we write ourselves," said Jin.

"We'll have actors," said Wanda.

"We'll have sets," said Julio.

"We'll have everything," said Talia.

"It is going to be incredibly great!" said Sally.

The members of the club were very excited.

READ & RESPOND

Author's Craft

Describe the mood the author creates by showing every member of the club speaking.

_____
_____

"I think our movie should have episodes," said Talia. "It can be like a TV series."

"That's a good idea," said Wanda. "But let's figure out the first episode before we think about any others. The first thing we need is a story!"

"I have a story here," said Jin. He took out a notebook and opened it up. "I wrote it this weekend when I was supposed to be raking the lawn. It is very exciting! I even drew a few pictures."

READ & RESPOND

Make Inferences

What can you infer about Jin based on what he says?

___
___
___

Julio thumbed through the pages of Jin's story. He read it quickly. He looked at the drawings. He liked the story! Already he had a clear mental picture of what the movie would look like.

Julio passed the notebook to Sally, and she started to read.

"This is fantastic!" said Julio. "It will make a great movie!"

"What's it about?" asked Talia.

"It's a story about a group of kids who go hiking," answered Julio. "They are walking along, very close to a river."

"Then Pablo falls in!" said Sally, looking up from the notebook. "He is messing around by the water's edge. He is running too fast. He trips and falls."

READ & RESPOND

Author's Craft

How does the author show Julio's personality? Give at least two examples from the text to support your answer.

"Yes! He falls right into some deep water. The river is very fast. It washes him downstream," said Julio.

"His friends are all scared," said Sally. "They can't see him anymore."

"They rush along the shore looking for him," said Julio. "The river has taken him. He washes up against a rock far downstream."

READ & RESPOND

Make Inferences

What would the movie club need to do in order to film the scene described on this page?

_____
_____

"That's not all!" added Jin. "When Pablo tries to swim out of the river, he sees a bear sitting on the bank."

"He's stuck," said Julio. "He can't stay in the water forever. He's too cold. He can't go out near the bear."

"He dips his head underwater and holds his breath. He hides behind the rock. After a while, the bear goes away," said Jin.

"His friends arrive," said Julio. "They pull him out."

Talia's eyes were wide. Her mouth was hanging open. Wanda was quiet.

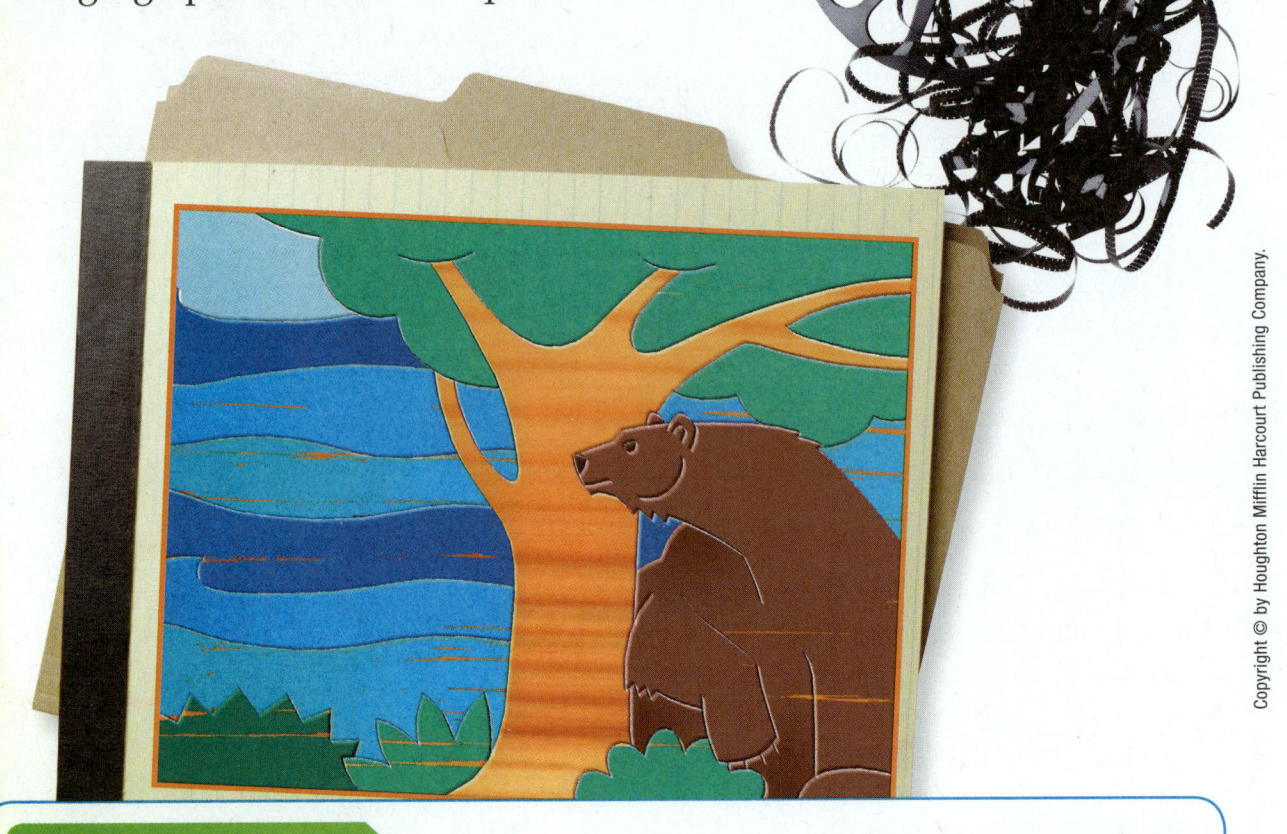

READ & RESPOND

Author's Craft

What is the mood at this point in the text? How does the author create that mood?

_____
_____
_____

"Wow!" said Talia. "That's quite a story. It sure would make a great movie."

"I can picture the scene with the bear!" said Sally. "We could have scary music in the background. The bear can growl and splash in the water."

"Pablo should look pale and exhausted when he finally gets pulled from the water," said Julio.

"Yes," said Jin. "That's perfect. Guess what? I already have some ideas for other episodes."

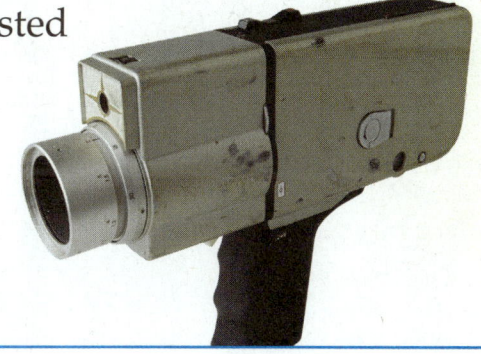

READ & RESPOND

Make Inferences

Why would Jin's story make a great movie? Explain.

_____

_____

"Jin, your story is great," said Wanda. "It would make a great movie. However, there are a few problems. First of all, we live in the city! The only wild animals here are pigeons and some stray cats. The only body of water is the public swimming pool. So how are we going to make a movie with a river and a bear?"

The others looked at each other blankly and scratched their heads.

Wanda continued. "Jin, save your story for Hollywood. For our video club, I'm afraid it's back to the drawing board!"

READ & RESPOND

Main Ideas and Details

What does Wanda mean when she says the video club has to go "back to the drawing board"?

_____
_____

Reread and Respond

1 How would you describe Julio and Sally?

_____
_____
_____

Hint
For clues, see pages 20 and 21.

2 How does the author show that this video club is not very experienced in planning or making movies?

_____
_____
_____

Hint
Look for clues on pages 19 to 23.

3 What clue does the author give early in the story that Wanda is the most practical of all the club members?

_____
_____
_____

Hint
See page 19.

4 What does Wanda mean when she tells Jin to save his story for Hollywood?

_____
_____
_____

Hint
Think about what happens in Hollywood.

A Trip to a Cave

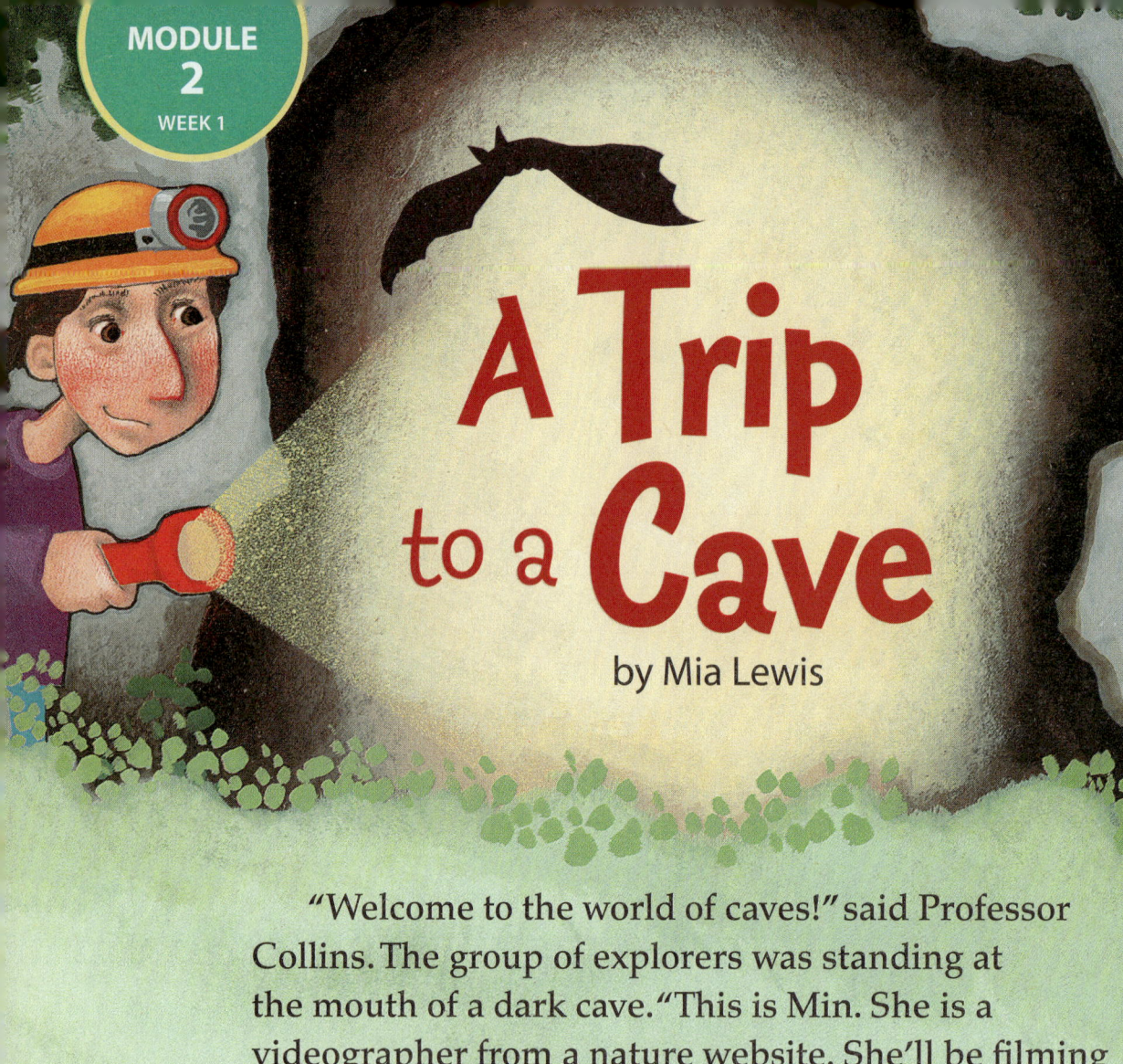

by Mia Lewis

"Welcome to the world of caves!" said Professor Collins. The group of explorers was standing at the mouth of a dark cave. "This is Min. She is a videographer from a nature website. She'll be filming our trip today."

"I think your website's cave exhibit is cool," said Hadley. He was one of the explorers.

"Hey, thanks, but I didn't make that exhibit. This is actually my first trip into a cave!" Min said.

"Well, don't worry," said Hadley. "You'll be fine."

READ & RESPOND Literary Elements

List the characters introduced on this page.

_____

_____

_____

"Cave explorers are called spelunkers," said Jordan. "The study of caves is called speleology."

"The terrain in these caves can be dangerous," said Professor Collins. "Some areas are not available for visitors to explore. We must be sure to follow the procedure for cave visitors."

"Which way do we go?" asked Lane. "All of the paths resemble each other." He looked nervous.

"Yes, that's why it's easy to get lost," warned the professor. "I know these caves, though. Let's just make sure we all stick together."

Professor Collins took the lead. The group started down the dark tunnel.

READ & RESPOND

Literary Elements

What is the setting of this story?

_____
_____
_____

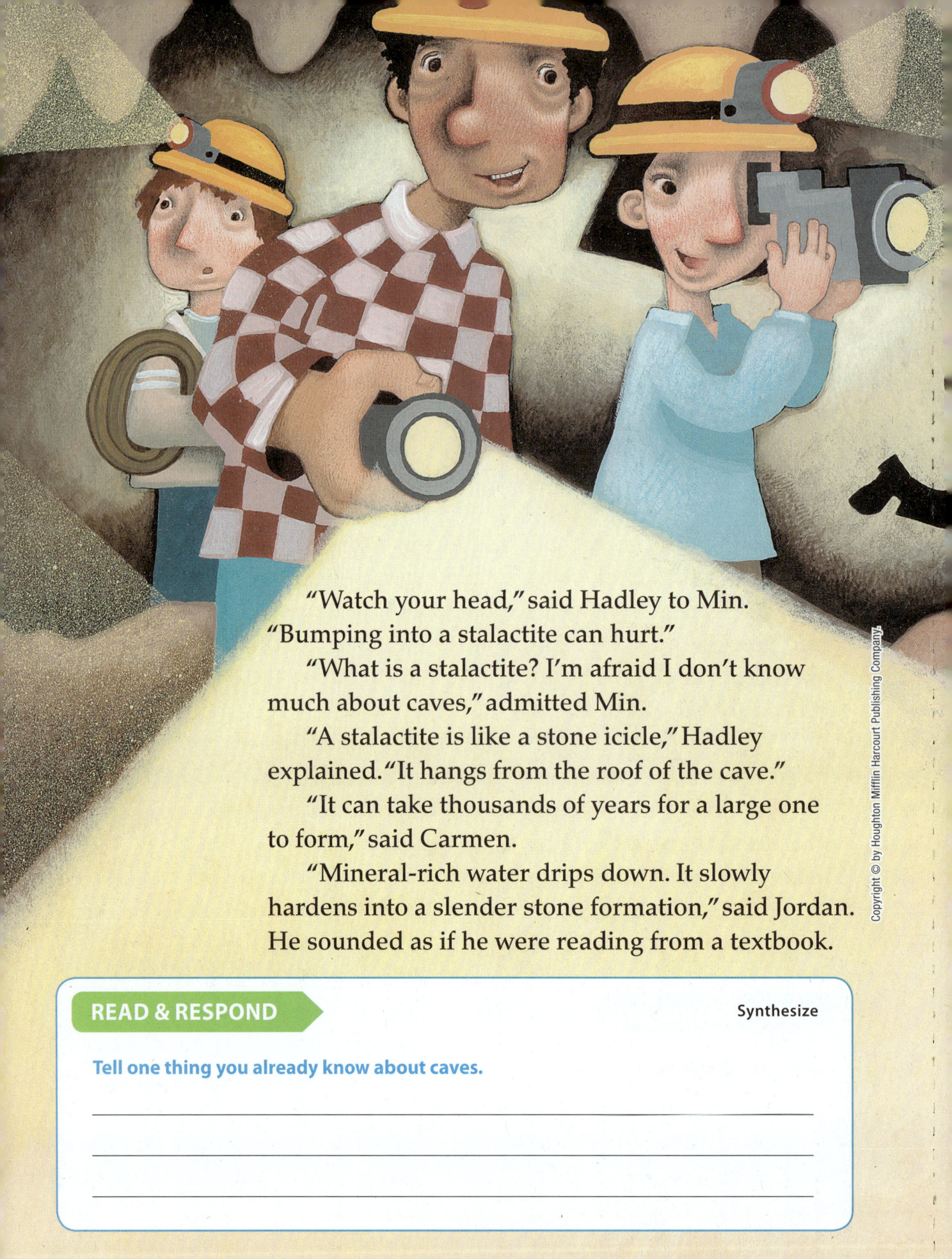

"Watch your head," said Hadley to Min. "Bumping into a stalactite can hurt."

"What is a stalactite? I'm afraid I don't know much about caves," admitted Min.

"A stalactite is like a stone icicle," Hadley explained. "It hangs from the roof of the cave."

"It can take thousands of years for a large one to form," said Carmen.

"Mineral-rich water drips down. It slowly hardens into a slender stone formation," said Jordan. He sounded as if he were reading from a textbook.

> **READ & RESPOND** Synthesize
>
> **Tell one thing you already know about caves.**
>
> _____
> _____
> _____

"Stalactites can be colored by different minerals," added the professor. "They can be red, blue, yellow, or other colors."

"Are these also stalactites on the cave floor?" asked Min.

"No! Those are stalagmites," explained Carmen. "They form from falling water droplets. I love them!"

Professor Collins told them that the rock forms weren't as strong as they looked. He warned them not to touch anything. Conserving the treasures of the cave was just as important as exploring it. Min got a good shot of the scene.

> **READ & RESPOND**
>
> Main Ideas and Details
>
> **Explain the difference between stalactites and stalagmites.**
>
> _____
> _____
> _____

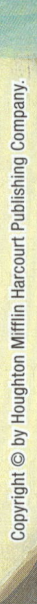

"Our website shows films of animals, too," said Min. "Do you think we'll see any?"

"Maybe," said Hadley. "We'll have to look closely. Most animals in caves are very small. There are a few larger ones as well."

"Many of the animals in caves are like the ones outside," said Carmen. "Still, there's one big difference. They're blind."

"They have adapted to the total darkness of the cave," said Jordan. "Sight wouldn't help them here. They use their other senses to get around."

READ & RESPOND

Synthesize

Did you learn any new information while reading this section? Explain.

_____
_____
_____

"Look! A crayfish!" said Carmen. "Cool!"

"Bats also live in caves," said Jordan. "They aren't blind, though, whatever people say."

"Aren't bats dangerous?" asked Lane. "Don't they carry diseases?"

"Well, some bats do carry rabies. It's best to avoid contact with them," warned Hadley. "Don't worry. Bats will want to avoid you, too!"

"Bats are helpful in checking the number of insects. They eat thousands every night," explained Jordan. "One small bat can eat about 600 insects an hour!"

READ & RESPOND

Literary Elements

How would you describe Lane?

_____
_____
_____

"Guys! Shine your flashlights up!" said Carmen.

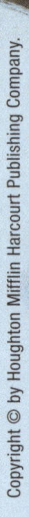

"What are those furry things up there?" gasped Lane.

"Hmm. I think those are gray bats," replied Jordan.

"Wow!" said Min. "Look how many there are! I hope we didn't disturb them. Do they usually move around so much?"

"Only when they are getting ready for a flight!" said Hadley.

"Quick!" said Carmen. "Everybody, duck! Make way for the bats!"

READ & RESPOND

Literary Elements

What happens at the end of this story?

_____
_____
_____

Reread and Respond

1 **What do spelunkers do?**

_____

_____

_____

> **Hint**
> For a clue, see page 27.

2 **How much does Min know about caves? Explain.**

_____

_____

_____

> **Hint**
> For clues, see pages 28 and 29.

3 **Write three words to describe Jordan.**

_____

_____

_____

> **Hint**
> Look for clues throughout the story.

4 **Compare Carmen and Lane. Which one is having more fun?**

_____

_____

_____

> **Hint**
> Look for clues throughout the story.

MODULE 2 WEEK 2

The Twin Twins

by Justin Shipley

Two best friends, Jamie and Kyle, head to the Little League World Series to see their favorite team, the Topeka Twins, play in the championship game.

Characters: Jamie, Ms. Thompson, Kyle, Ticket Taker, Manager, Chase Conway

Scene I

Setting: The interior of Ms. Thompson's car.

Jamie: Thanks for driving us to the Little League World Series, Ms. Thompson!

Ms. Thompson: No problem, Jamie! I know how much basketball means to you and Kyle.

Kyle: Mom, please! You're embarrassing me! The Little League World Series is not basketball.

READ & RESPOND

Elements of Drama

Where does Scene I take place? What clues in the text help you to know?

_____
_____
_____

Jamie: The Topeka Twins are our favorite baseball team, and Kyle looks exactly like their star pitcher, Chase Conway! *(teasing Kyle)* Now if only you could throw like him.

Kyle: Too bad Chase is hurt. I'd love to see him play!

(The car comes to a stop outside of a baseball stadium.)

Ms. Thompson: I'd hate for you to come all the way here only to miss the game. Do you have your tickets?

Kyle: Of course we have our tickets! I'm going to leave my jacket in the car. Doesn't look like rain today.

(Kyle puts his coat in the car and shuts the door.)

Jamie: Come on, Chase. It's time for your big game!

READ & RESPOND

Elements of Drama

Write one example of a stage direction found on this page.

Scene II

(Moments later, Jamie and Kyle approach the Ticket Taker.)

Ticket Taker: Tickets, please.

Kyle: Jamie, give him our tickets.

Jamie: *(looking at Kyle in surprise)* I thought you said you would hang on to them.

Kyle: Oh, no. I left them in my rain jacket! In the car!

Ticket Taker: Sorry, boys. I can't let you in. The game is sold out.

(Jamie and Kyle step out of line, dejected.)

Kyle: I'm so sorry, Jamie. I can't believe I bungled holding the tickets.

Jamie: Let's see if someone has an extra ticket.

READ & RESPOND

Elements of Drama

How do you know who Kyle and Jamie are talking to?

_____
_____
_____

36

(Kyle and Jamie circle the stadium looking for an extra ticket, with no luck.)

Kyle: Oh, man. We're going to miss the game.

(The Topeka Twins Manager appears from inside the stadium and waves to Kyle.)

Manager: Chase! Over here!

Jamie: Huh? He's not . . . *(Kyle covers Jamie's mouth and turns him around.)*

Kyle: He thinks I'm Chase Conway! If I pretend to be Chase, I could get us into the game!

Jamie: But that's a lie. And you can't throw like Chase.

Kyle: I wouldn't have to throw like Chase. He's injured, remember? Just follow my lead. *(to the manager)* Yeah, it's me, Chase! I'm coming!

READ & RESPOND

Elements of Drama

Explain how the dialogue on this page shows that the manager thinks Kyle is Chase Conway.

_____

_____

Scene III

Setting: Inside the Topeka Twins' locker room.

Kyle: *(looking around)* Whoa! Cool!

Jamie: Quit fooling, Chase! *(Jamie elbows Kyle, reminding him to keep up his performance.)*

Manager: *(points to Jamie)* Who's your friend, Chase?

Kyle: Him? That's my, uh . . . my new trainer, Jamie!

Manager: So this is the new trainer! *(shaking Jamie's hand)* Thank you for preparing Chase for today's game. We're glad he'll be able to play without any discomfort!

Kyle: *(shocked)* What? I'm playing?

Manager: Nobody told you? You're starting today.

(The Manager leaves. Kyle and Jamie look worried.)

> **READ & RESPOND**
>
> Main Idea and Details
>
> **Why are Kyle and Jamie worried?**
> _____
> _____
> _____

Kyle: Jamie, I can't play like Chase.

Jamie: I guess you'll have to just tell him the truth.

Kyle: But I've already lied. And then we won't be able to see the game.

(*The Manager returns.*)

Manager: Okay, Chase, ready to go?

Kyle: Uh, sir, I'm not Chase Conway.

Manager: Come on, Chase. Stop playing around.

Kyle: No, I'm really not Chase. I just look like him.

Manager: What? You're not Chase? Who are you?

Kyle: We figured if you thought I was Chase, you'd let us into the game.

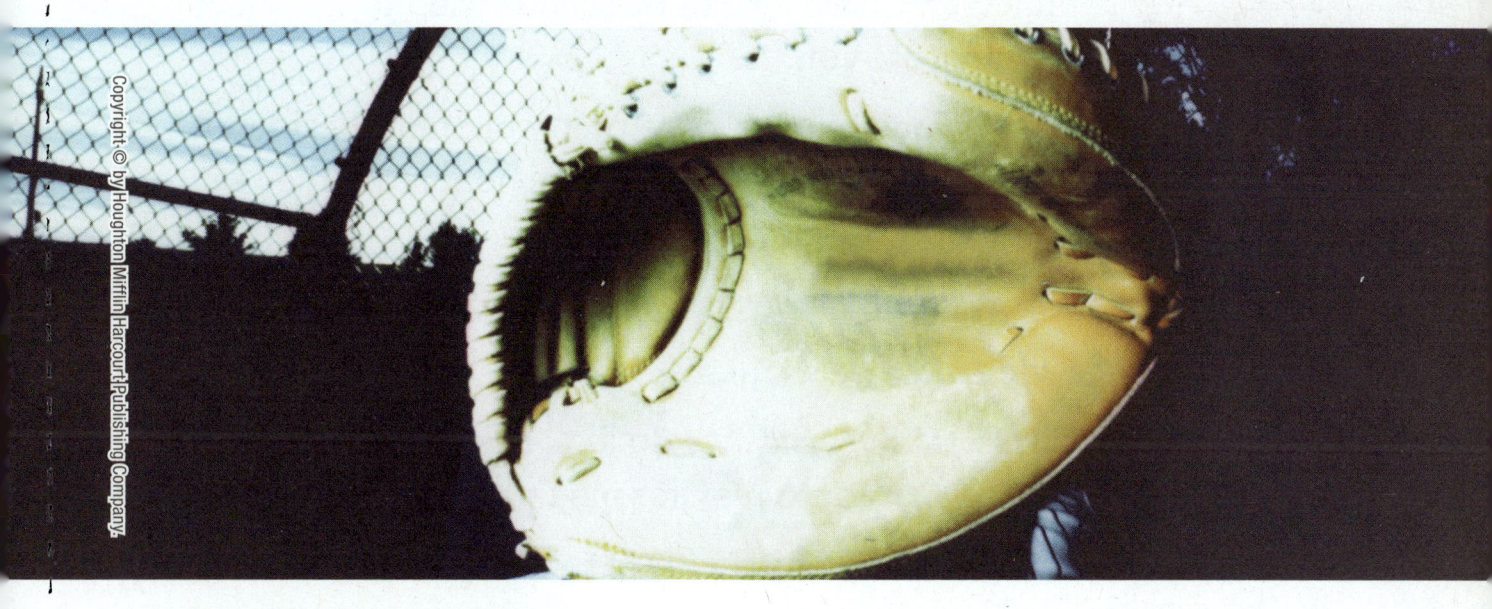

READ & RESPOND

Elements of Drama

How does the dialogue on this page help you understand how the manager feels?

Manager: I see. Well, boys, I'm afraid I'm going to have to ask you to leave.

Chase: That won't be necessary.

(All three turn around to see Chase Conway enter.)

Kyle & Jamie: Chase Conway!

Manager: Chase, one of these kids tried to impersonate you.

Chase: Then they must be pretty big fans. Besides, it takes guts to tell the truth. I'd be honored if they sat in my own personal fan section.

(Chase extends his hands, brandishing two tickets.)

Kyle & Jamie: Thanks, Chase!

Chase: (to Kyle) Say, we do look alike. Are you sure you don't want to play for me today?

Kyle: (smiling) No, thanks. I think I'll just be Kyle.

READ & RESPOND

Elements of Drama

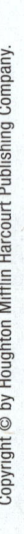

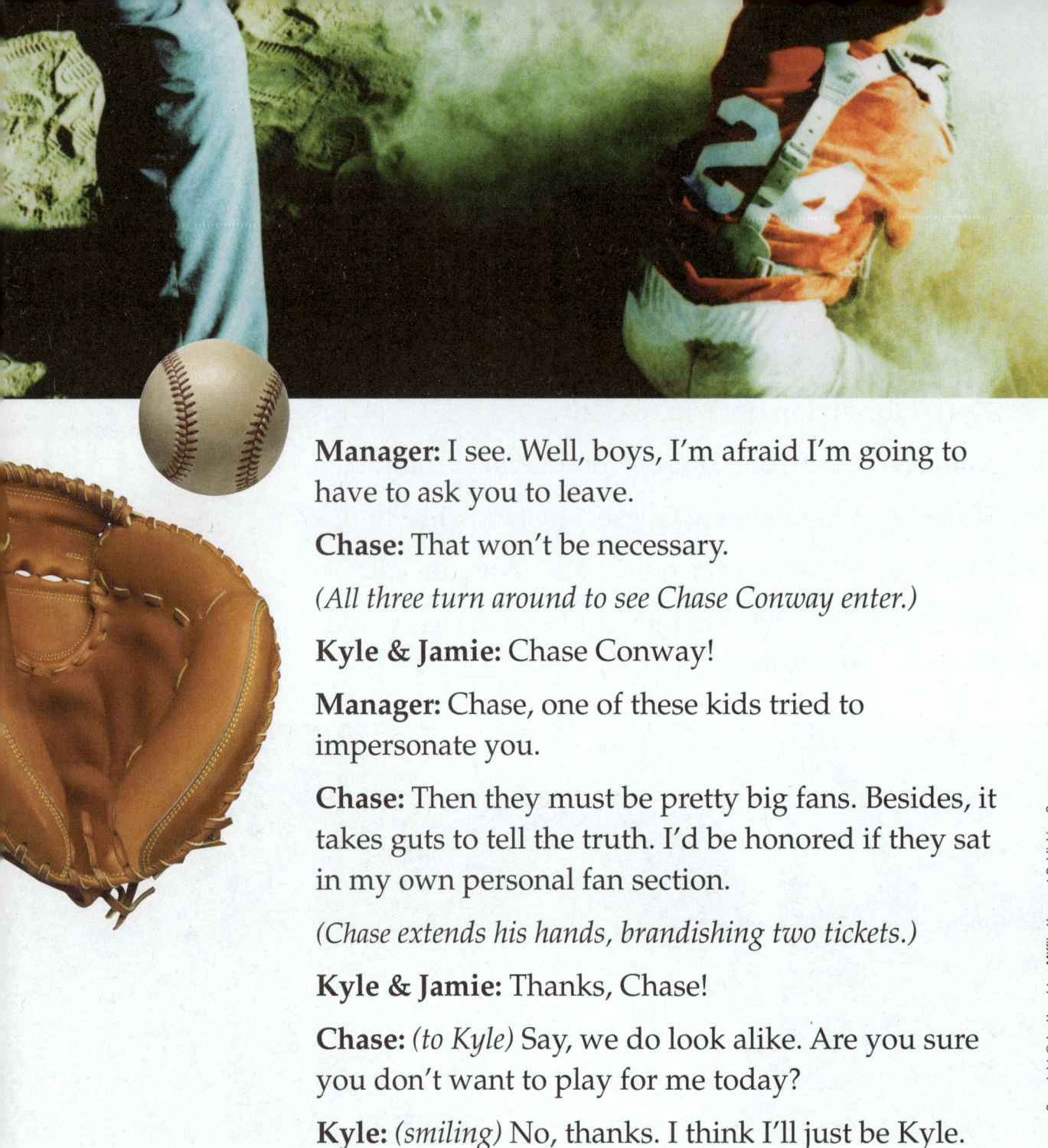

Who enters for the first time on this page? Why is this character important?

_____
_____
_____

Reread and Respond

1 How does Ms. Thompson embarrass Kyle?
_____
_____
_____

> **Hint**
> For a clue, see page 34.

2 What happened to Kyle and Jamie's tickets?
_____
_____
_____

> **Hint**
> For a clue, see page 36.

3 How do Kyle and Jamie feel after the Manager tells Kyle he'll be playing in the big game?
_____
_____
_____

> **Hint**
> For clues, see pages 38 and 39.

4 What does Kyle learn by revealing to the Manager that he is not Chase?
_____
_____
_____

> **Hint**
> For a clue, see page 40.

MODULE 2 WEEK 3

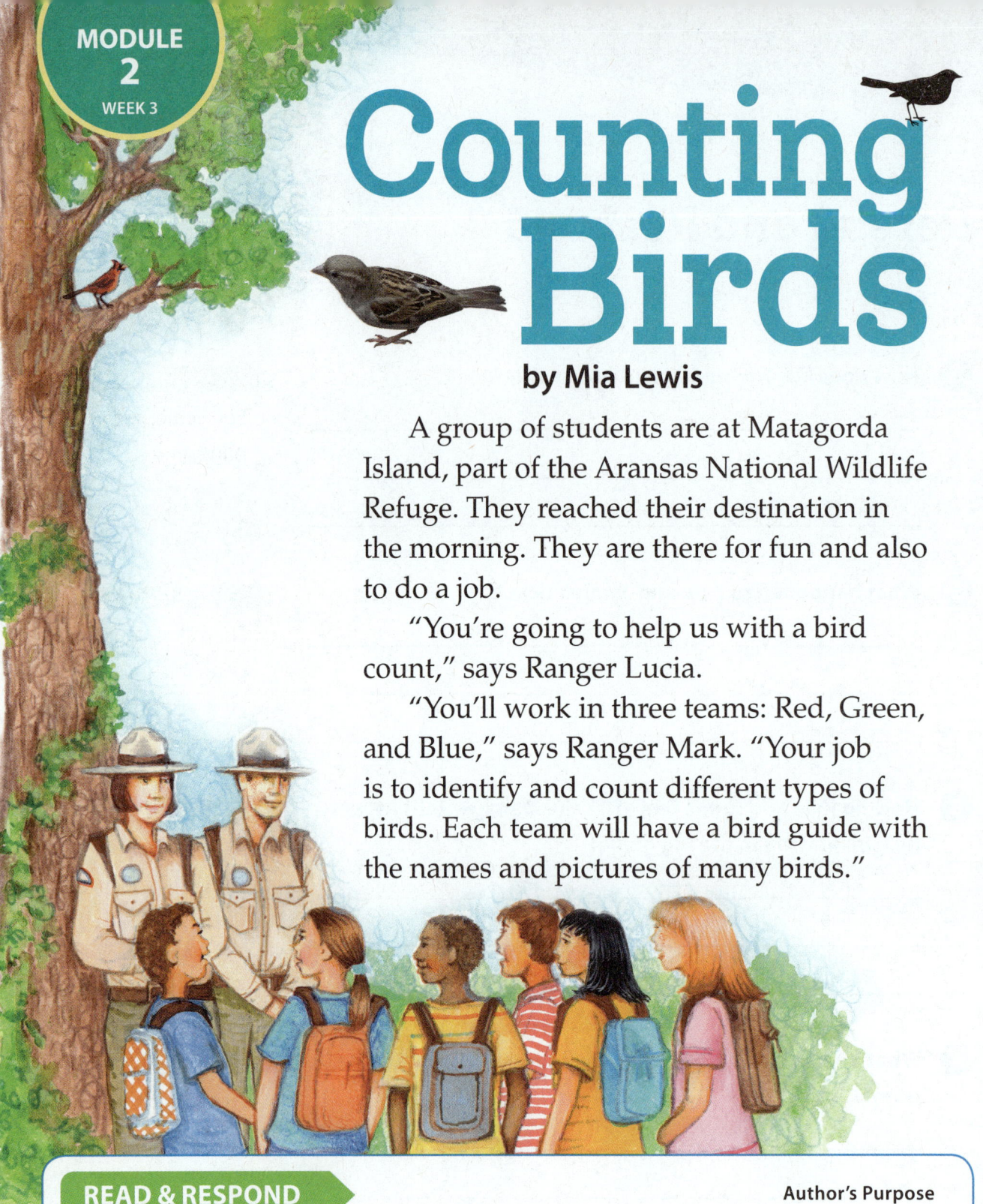

Counting Birds

by Mia Lewis

A group of students are at Matagorda Island, part of the Aransas National Wildlife Refuge. They reached their destination in the morning. They are there for fun and also to do a job.

"You're going to help us with a bird count," says Ranger Lucia.

"You'll work in three teams: Red, Green, and Blue," says Ranger Mark. "Your job is to identify and count different types of birds. Each team will have a bird guide with the names and pictures of many birds."

READ & RESPOND

Author's Purpose

Why do you think this author wrote about students at the wildlife refuge?

_____
_____
_____

42

"There's a special way to count," says Lucia. "Only record the highest number of birds you see together at one time. Here's how it works. Let's say you see a group of three sparrows. You write that down. Later you see a group of five sparrows. You write that down. Then you see a group of two sparrows. You do not write that down because you have already seen a larger group."

Mark added, "Your record book would say *Sparrows: 3, 5. High count = 5*. Only the 5 goes into the final count. That way you're sure that you haven't counted the same birds more than once."

READ & RESPOND

Ask and Answer Questions

Do you understand how the teams are supposed to count? What can you do to help you understand this information?

_____

_____

"Got it?" asks Mark. "Good! Off you go. Meet us back here in one hour."

The three teams spread out to different areas of the park. Joe, Darlene, and Bill are on the Red Team. The first thing they do is sit down with their guidebook. They read the tips with insights about the most effective ways to identify birds using the way they fly and their size, coloring, and songs.

"I can help identify the birds," says Joe. "My parents are bird watchers."

"Great!" says Darlene. "Let's go."

READ & RESPOND

Ask and Answer Questions

Write one question you have about the text so far.

_____
_____
_____

Emma, Josh, and Tia are on the Blue Team. They start out without looking at the guidebook. Pretty soon they see some birds.

"Look!" says Emma. "Little yellow birds!"

"Does anyone know what they are?" asks Tia.

"Not me," says Josh. "That's an incredibly bright yellow. Let's see if we can find them in the book."

"Check this picture," says Tia. "I think these are American goldfinches."

READ & RESPOND

Author's Purpose

Do you think this text is more interesting or more entertaining so far? Explain.

_____
_____
_____

The Green Team is walking toward the water. Sam, Beth, and Alec stop when they hear a honking noise. They turn to look and see a huge bird standing in the water.

"Wow!" says Alec. "Look at that giant bird! It must be as tall as a person."

"Look in the guidebook," says Sam. "Let's see what it is."

"It's a whooping crane!" says Beth.

"I think you're right," says Sam. "It's mostly white like the bird in the picture. It also has the same black and red patch on its head."

READ & RESPOND

Main Ideas and Details

How does the Green Team identify the crane?

_____
_____
_____

"The guide says that whooping cranes stand nearly five feet tall," says Beth. "They have a wingspan of seven feet."

"They travel in pairs or as a family," says Sam.

"Look at this," says Alec, pointing to the page in the book. "They are an endangered species. They are in trouble."

"That's why refuges like this are required. The cranes need them so that they can make a comeback," says Beth. "Hey, guys, let's see if we can find the whole family."

READ & RESPOND

Ask and Answer Questions

Write one question about a bird from the text that you want to know more about.

_____
_____
_____

Very soon, the hour is up. The teams meet back up with the rangers.

"We saw two quails," says Joe for the Red Team.

"The Blue Team saw four American goldfinches," says Emma.

"We saw five whooping cranes," says Alec. "The Green Team wins!"

"Yes," says Ranger Lucia. "All the information the teams gathered is useful. It will help scientists understand how birds adapt to changes in their environment."

"Good job everyone!" says Ranger Mark. "Come back next year and help us count birds again!"

READ & RESPOND

Author's Purpose

Why do you think the author wrote this article? Explain.

_____
_____
_____

Reread and Respond

1. How do the bird guides help the students identify birds?
   _____
   _____
   _____

   Hint
   For clues, see pages 44 through 47.

2. Why are wildlife refuges important?
   _____
   _____
   _____

   Hint
   For clues, see page 47.

3. Why do you think the rangers divide the students into three teams?
   _____
   _____
   _____

   Hint
   Think about the job that the students are going to do.

4. Is the trip to the wildlife refuge a success? Explain.
   _____
   _____
   _____

   Hint
   Look at the first and last pages of the story.

An Ocean Learner

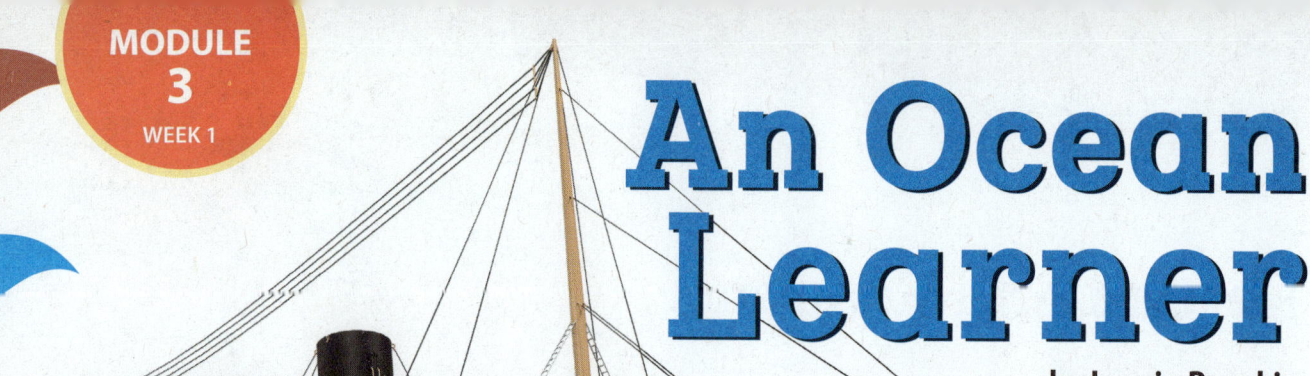

by Laurie Rozakis

Juan stared at the open cartons. How could he fit four months of his life into them? He had to, though. That was all Mom and Dad would let him take along.

"There's not much room on a ship," Mom had said.

The Garcias weren't taking a vacation. Mom and Dad were going to be teachers for School at Sea. High school students would spend two months on the ship. They would take all their classes there. Juan was going with his parents.

READ & RESPOND Make and Confirm Predictions

Do you think Juan will like living on the ship? Why, or why not?

_____

_____

Mom and Dad were thrilled. Juan did not like the idea one bit.

For weeks, the family prepared. They packed clothing, cameras, and books.

Mom and Dad spent hours writing lesson plans. Dad was a math teacher. Mom's specialty was science.

Juan spent the time complaining. "I am not a fish," he said. "I live on land. Why are you wrecking my life?"

"You'll love going to school at sea," said Mom. "You'll see how much you'll enjoy—"

Juan interrupted Mom before she could go on. "I want to go to *my* school. I don't want to be trapped on some boat."

READ & RESPOND

Figurative Language

The narrator says the Juan "did not like the idea one bit." Is this an example of figurative language? Explain.

_____

_____

Finally, the big day came. The Garcias arrived at the dock. Juan staggered unsteadily as he lugged a suitcase. Gripping the handle was making his fingers feel numb.

The ship was larger than Juan had expected. Maybe it wouldn't tip over and sink in a storm after all.

He wasn't going to be the only young kid on board. Another boy stood nearby. The other boy looked excited.

"That must be Ted Blake and his parents," said Dad.

"See?" said Mom. "You'll have friends. You're sharing a cabin with Ted."

Juan just grunted. He wanted his *land* friends.

READ & RESPOND

Figurative Language

What sensory words on this page help you feel what Juan is feeling? Explain.

_____

_____

Juan and Ted found their cabin. It was so tiny! The furniture was odd, too. The beds were built into the walls. Chairs were bolted to the floor. "Does this mean the boat could turn over on its side?" Juan asked.

"Not a chance," said Ted. "Big ships are pretty steady."

School began the next day. The teachers' kids had their own classes. There, Juan and Ted met Kim.

"What a great way to go to school," said Kim. "Here, when we study dolphins, we get to see them."

Dolphins? Juan loved dolphins. Maybe this ocean school would be okay.

READ & RESPOND

Make and Confirm Predictions

How do Juan's feelings begin to change in this part of the story? Is your earlier prediction correct so far, or do you need to adjust it?

_____

_____

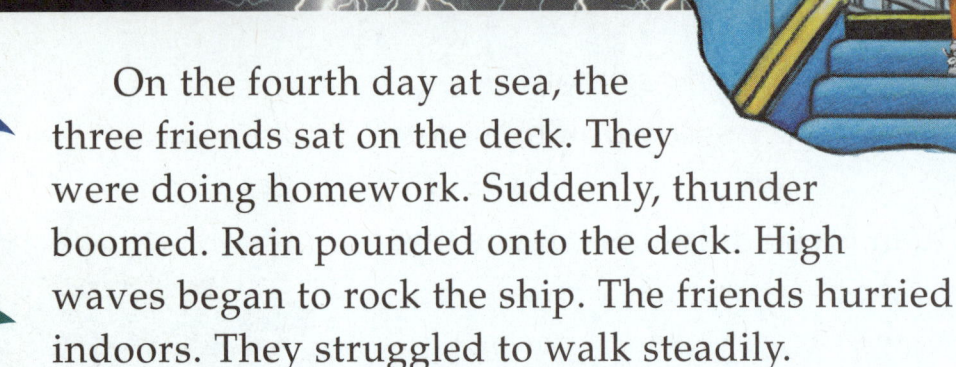

On the fourth day at sea, the three friends sat on the deck. They were doing homework. Suddenly, thunder boomed. Rain pounded onto the deck. High waves began to rock the ship. The friends hurried indoors. They struggled to walk steadily.

At last the three reached Juan and Ted's cabin. "Whew!" said Ted. "How could a storm come up that fast?"

Juan smiled. He knew the answer! "A warm front and a cold front came together," he said. "It was on the weather map we studied earlier."

"Cool!" said Kim. "We get to live what we're learning."

READ & RESPOND

Figurative Language

What examples of onomatopoeia do you see on this page? How do they help you picture what is happening in the story?

_____

_____

54

In a few hours, the sun had dried everything out. The three friends went back outside.

Mom came over. "Are you ready for science class?" she asked.

"We're way ahead of you," said Ted. "Our science class started hours ago."

For the first time in weeks, Juan felt like laughing, and he did. "Yes, Mom," he said. "We learned a thing or two about weather maps today."

Mom did not say "I told you so." She didn't have to. Juan had already figured out that he was going to a pretty good school.

READ & RESPOND

Make and Confirm Predictions

How does Juan feel about living on the ship now? Was your prediction correct?

_____
_____
_____

The World's Biggest Store: The Ocean!

We get more than just fish from the ocean. Sea plants and animals are used in medicine, toothpaste, shampoo, fertilizer, and ice cream.

The Place to Live

More than half the people in the world live within sixty miles of an ocean. That is more than than 3.4 billion people! Close to half of all Americans live near the coast.

Ocean Facts

Area	The area of our oceans is 140 million square miles. That's more than two-thirds of Earth's surface.
Deepest point	The Mariana Trench in the western Pacific is more than five miles deep.
Biggest animal	The blue whale is the largest animal on Earth. It is bigger than the biggest dinosaur ever was.

READ & RESPOND Main Ideas and Details

How do these facts help you understand more about what you can learn from going to school on a ship?

_____
_____

Reread and Respond

1 Which of the two settings is more important in this story? Why?

_____
_____
_____

> **Hint**
> For clues, look at pages 50, 53, 54, and 55.

2 At first, how are Juan's feelings about School at Sea different from Ted's?

_____
_____
_____

> **Hint**
> For clues, look at pages 50, 52, and 53.

3 How does Juan's attitude change during the story?

_____
_____
_____

> **Hint**
> For clues, look at pages 51, 53, and 55.

4 What is the most important thing that Juan learns in the story?

_____
_____
_____

> **Hint**
> For clues, look at pages 53, 54, and 55.

Sojourner Truth

Speaker for Equal Rights

by Duncan Searl

Her Early Life

Sojourner Truth fought for equal rights for all people. She did this because she knew what it was like to have no rights.

She was born enslaved in New York in 1797. Her name then was Isabella Baumfree. Even as a child, Isabella had to work hard. She was sold away from her family at the age of nine. As she grew up, she was sold again many times. She was often beaten by cruel masters. In time, she married and had five children. Several of her children were sold.

READ & RESPOND

Central Idea

Do the title and subtitle have clues about the central idea of this text? Explain.

_____
_____
_____

Isabella Finds Freedom and Strength

By the 1800s, many states had passed laws against slavery. New York's enslaved people became free in 1827. Isabella Baumfree's owner promised to free her. He went back on his promise, so Isabella escaped to freedom. She took her baby, Sophia, with her.

A kind couple took Isabella in. With their help, she went to court to get her son Peter back. He had been sold to a slave owner in the South. It took a year for Isabella to win her case. At last she got her son back!

READ & RESPOND

Central Idea

Who is Isabella Baumfree? How do details about her life support the central idea?

_____
_____
_____

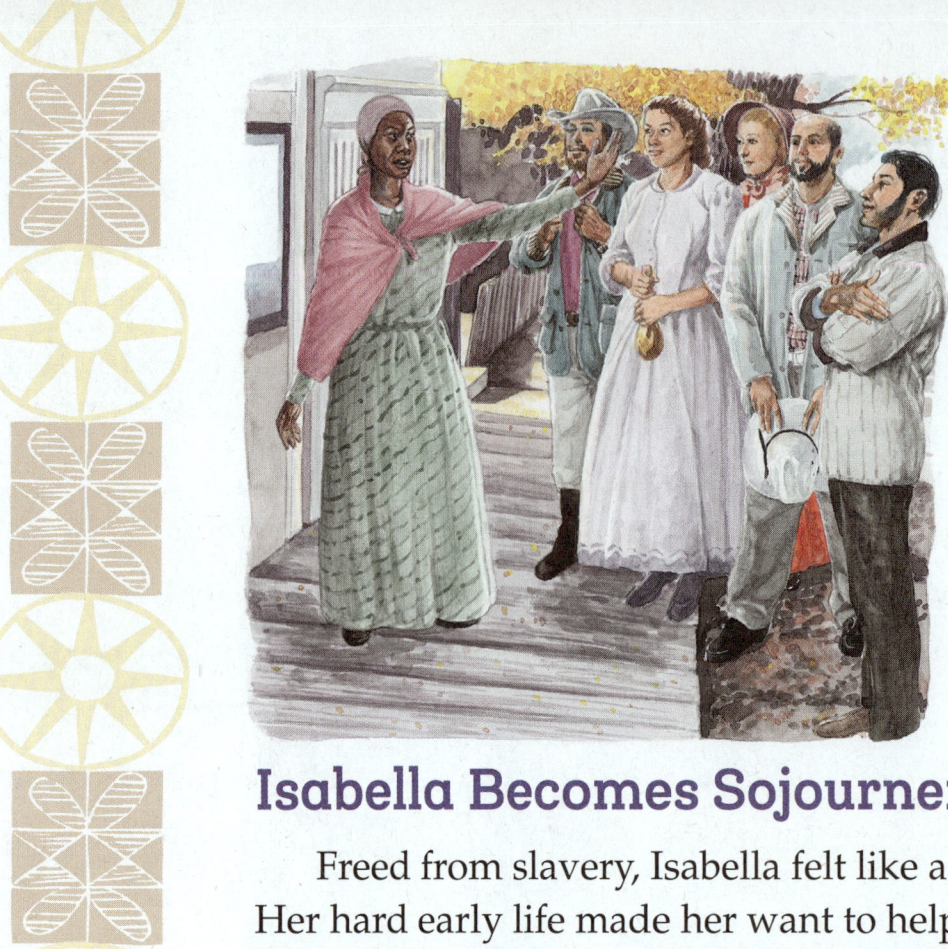

Isabella Becomes Sojourner Truth

Freed from slavery, Isabella felt like a new person. Her hard early life made her want to help others. To do that, she gave speeches. In her speeches, she shared her beliefs.

Isabella was an effective speaker. People listened closely. Her words gave them courage and hope. She never made much money. For food, she was often dependent on the kindness of others.

In 1843, she changed her name. She became Sojourner Truth. A sojourner is a traveler. Sojourner Truth felt that this new name showed what she wanted to do with her life.

READ & RESPOND

Central Idea

Explain why Isabella chose to change her name to Sojourner Truth.

_____
_____
_____

Sojourner Truth, Abolitionist

At that time, many people were trying to end slavery. These people were called abolitionists. Sojourner Truth joined the abolitionist cause. She knew that her words against slavery would have great meaning. After all, she had been enslaved. She gave speeches on this issue.

Sojourner Truth met other abolitionists. One was Frederick Douglass. He had also escaped slavery. Douglass was one of the great abolitionist speakers.

In 1850, Sojourner Truth published her life story. She had never learned to write. She couldn't even read. So a friend wrote down her words.

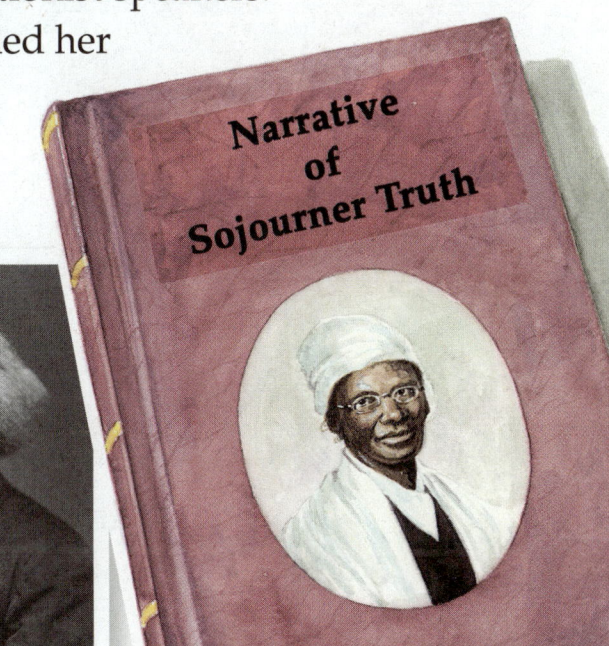

Frederick Douglass spoke out against slavery.

> **READ & RESPOND**
>
> Central Idea
>
> **Sojourner Truth and Frederick Douglass both escaped slavery. How do you think this helped them as abolitionist speakers?**
>
> _____
> _____

Women Deserve Rights, Too

Many abolitionists were women. However, women had few rights themselves. Only men could vote. There was no exception to that rule. Only men could hold most jobs. Many people thought that women were too weak to work.

Not Sojourner Truth! She knew how hard women could work. She began to urge women to claim their rights. In 1851, she spoke at the Women's Rights Convention in Akron, Ohio.

"Look at my arm!" she cried in her huge voice. "I have plowed and planted and gathered into barns." She added, "I could work as much and eat as much as a man—when I could get it." For the rest of her life, she kept speaking out.

> **READ & RESPOND**
>
> Central Idea
>
> **Why did Sojourner Truth urge women to gain their rights?**
> _____
> _____
> _____

After Slavery Ended

In time, one of Sojourner Truth's dreams came true. Slavery was ended in the U.S. in 1865. Sojourner Truth kept working to help African Americans. She helped ex-slaves settle in the West. She tried to get land grants for many of them.

She did not see women gain the right to vote. That did not happen until 1920. Sojourner Truth died in 1883. She was 86. A strong, brave woman, Truth spent her life helping others.

READ & RESPOND

Central Idea

Why did the author include details about the work Sojourner Truth did after slavery ended?

_____

_____

Did You Know?

- Sojourner Truth grew up speaking Dutch. She did not learn English until she was nine.

- By the time Sojourner Truth was 13, she had been sold three times.

- In the early 1850s, Sojourner Truth journeyed through 22 states. Everywhere she went, she spoke against slavery.

- Sojourner Truth was six feet tall and very strong. She wasn't afraid of angry crowds!

- Sojourner Truth met Abraham Lincoln in 1864. They had a long talk.

READ & RESPOND

Central Idea

How do these facts help you know Sojourner Truth better?

_____
_____
_____

Reread and Respond

1 What issues were important to Sojourner Truth?
_____
_____
_____

> **Hint**
> For clues, see pages 58, 61, and 62.

2 What point does the author make about the life of Sojourner Truth? What evidence does he provide?
_____
_____
_____

> **Hint**
> Clues are on every page!

3 What words would you use to describe Sojourner Truth?
_____
_____
_____

> **Hint**
> Your answers to questions 1 and 2 should help you.

4 In what ways do people like Sojourner Truth help make our world better?
_____
_____
_____

> **Hint**
> Your answer to question 3 should help you.

MODULE 3 WEEK 3

No Tea for Me!

by Laurie Rozakis

"The king taxed paper. The king taxed glass. The king taxed paint. Now the king is taxing tea! We won't pay it!" the American colonists shouted. "We want the king to repeal the unfair taxes!"

Many colonists liked to drink tea. They didn't think the tea tax was fair because they didn't get to decide how the tax money was spent. So, many people just stopped drinking tea. Britain lowered the tax a little but would not take away all the tax. The colonists got more and more angry. They decided not to buy any tea at all.

READ & RESPOND

Main Ideas and Details

Why did the colonists think the tea tax was unfair?

_____
_____
_____

We Won't Pay

It was December 16, 1773. More than 7,000 angry colonists stood on the Boston dock. Three big British ships were in the harbor. They carried a lot of tea. The governor told the people to let the ships unload the tea. The colonists objected to the order.

The colonists were very angry. If the ships were unloaded, the colonists would have to pay the tea tax. They wanted the ships to leave without unloading. A leader named Samuel Adams held meetings. He told the people not to let the ships unload. The people cheered!

READ & RESPOND

Text Structure

Reread this page carefully and notice how the events are organized. What text structure is the author using?

_____
_____

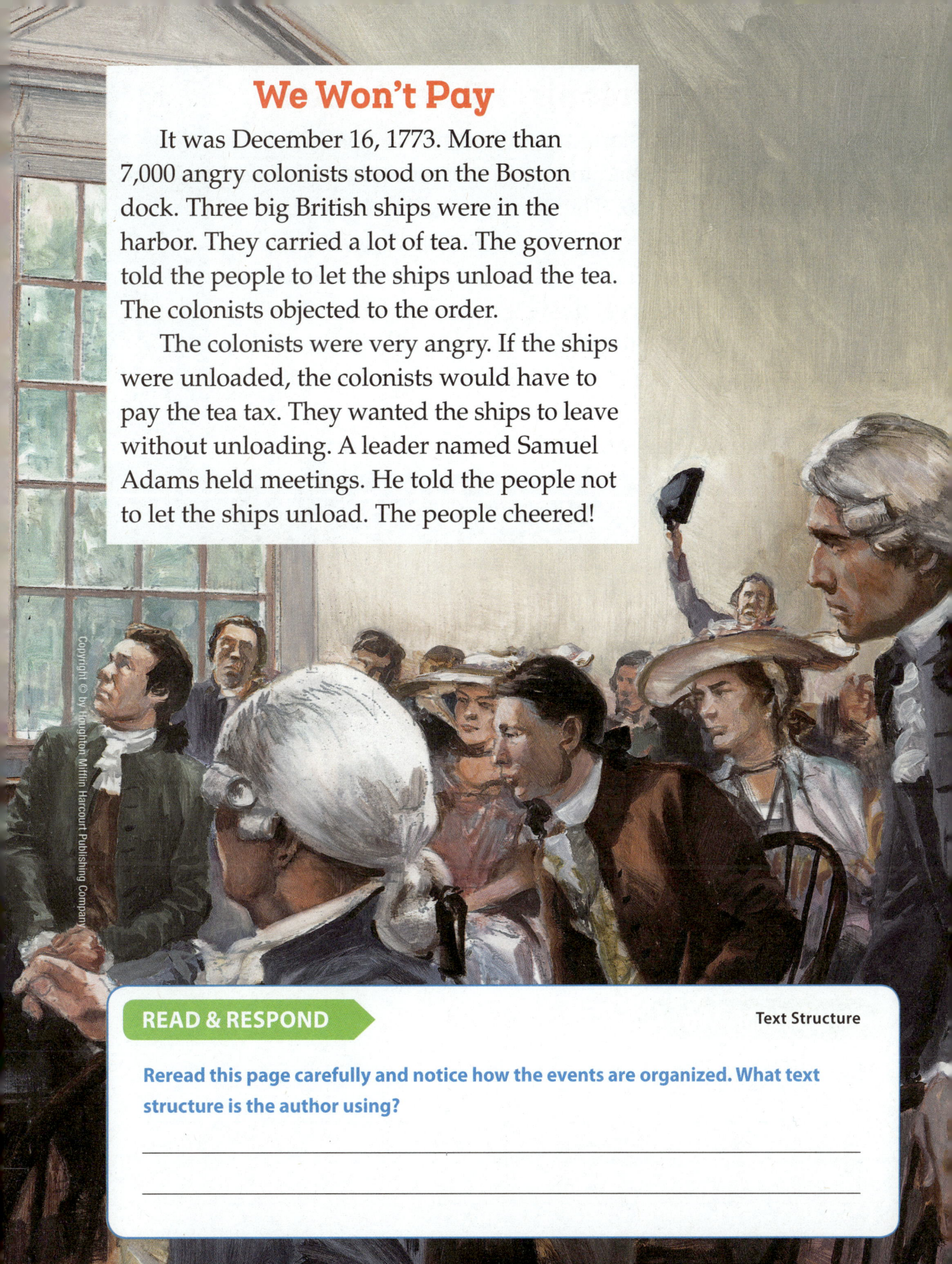

The Colonists Take Action

One ship started to sail away. But the British said the ship had to stay in port until the colonists paid the tea tax. The colonists made a bold plan.

That night, rebellious colonists disguised themselves. They dressed as American Indians. They rubbed coal dust all over their faces. They did not want the British to know who they were.

They carried small axes. Yelling very loudly, the colonists stormed the docks. Groups of colonists ran onto the three ships at the same time.

READ & RESPOND

Text Structure

How does the text structure help readers understand what happened?

_____
_____
_____

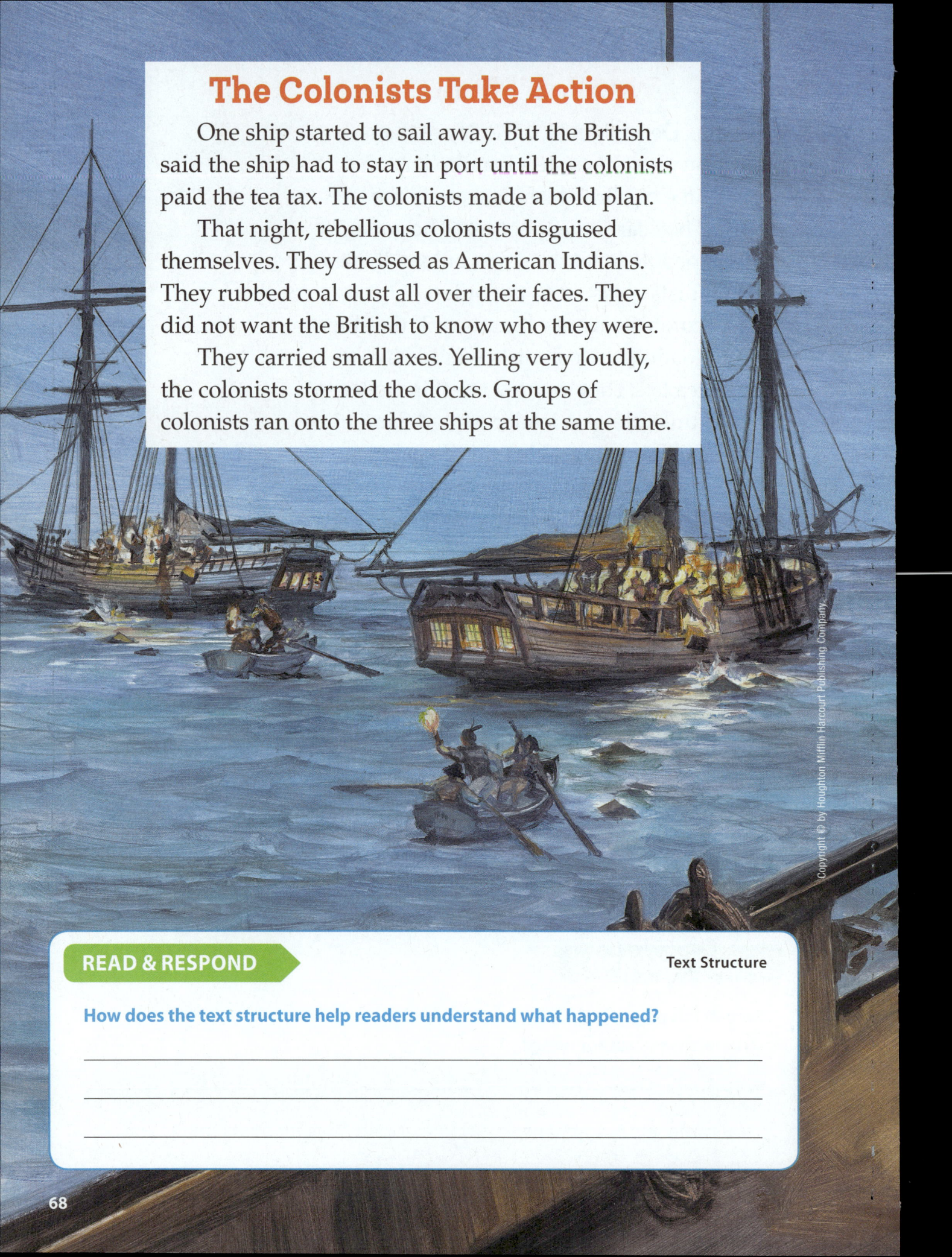

A Bold Tea Party

The men got the keys to the storage hatches. They unlocked the doors. They grabbed the chests of tea. They chopped holes in the tea chests. That way, the chests would not float in the water like corks. Their axes crashed into the dry wood. Then they tossed the chests of tea over the sides of the boats.

Some of the tea was still floating in the water the next day. The men beat the crates with paddles to make them sink. They did not want any of the tea to be saved.

READ & RESPOND

Text Structure

What do the transition words on this page tell you about the text structure?

_____
_____
_____

The British Punish the Colonists

British ships in the harbor left the colonists alone. The British king did not. Back in England, King George was very, very angry. He did not like this "tea party" at all. He did not like the way the colonists had acted. Their actions did not have any benefit for him or his country.

The king quickly closed Boston Harbor. That meant that no goods at all could reach Boston by ship. King George also took many powers away from the colonists.

READ & RESPOND Main Ideas and Details

Explain why the king was angry at the colonists.

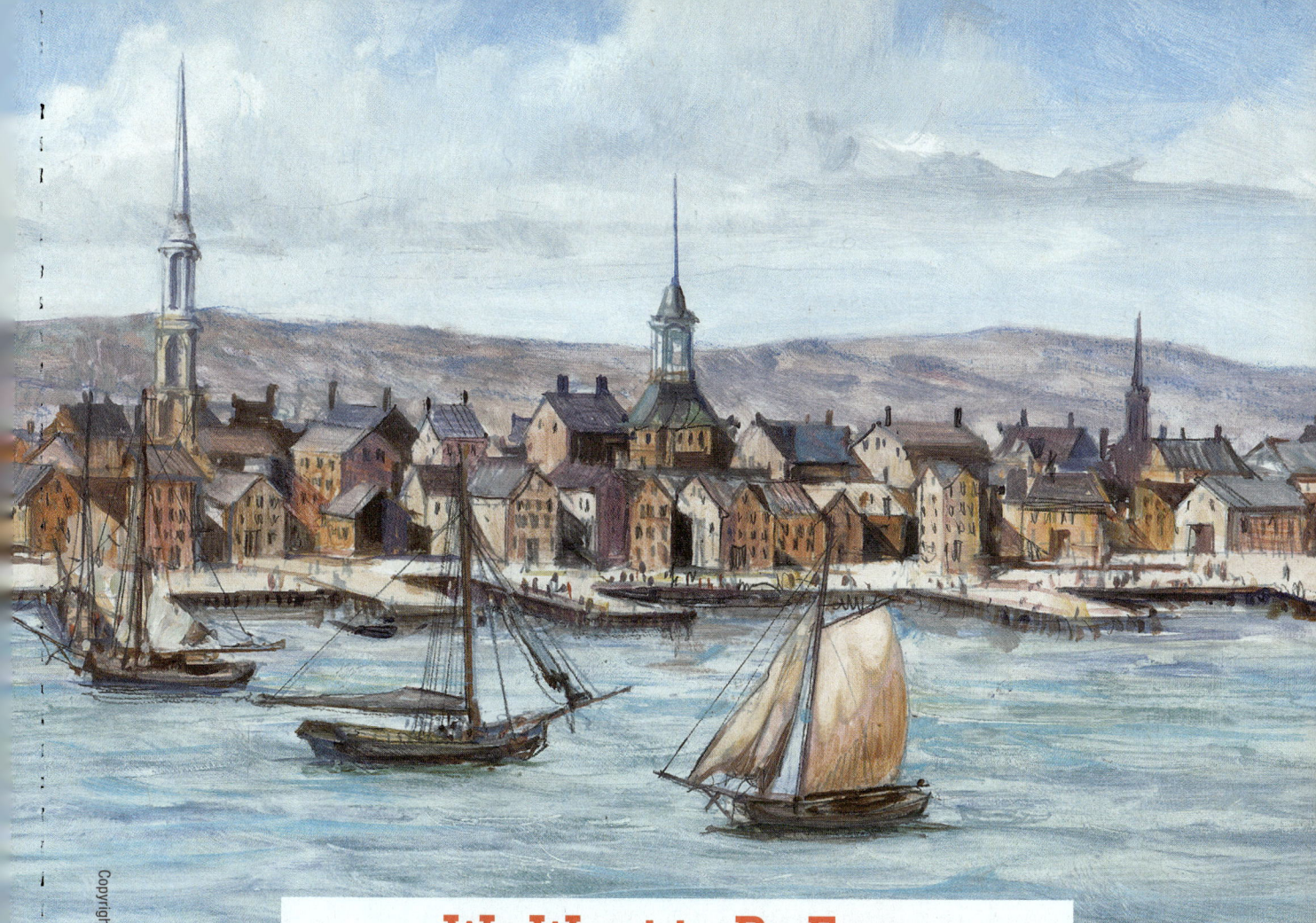

We Want to Be Free

Most colonists were pleased about the Boston Tea Party. They felt the rebels had done the right thing. Their act had many advantages. It helped unite the colonists. It showed the king that the colonists would take a stand. It showed they would not pay unfair taxes.

The battle for American freedom had begun.

READ & RESPOND

Text Structure

Do you think the author chose an effective text structure to share the information in this text? Explain.

_____
_____

"Liberty Tea"

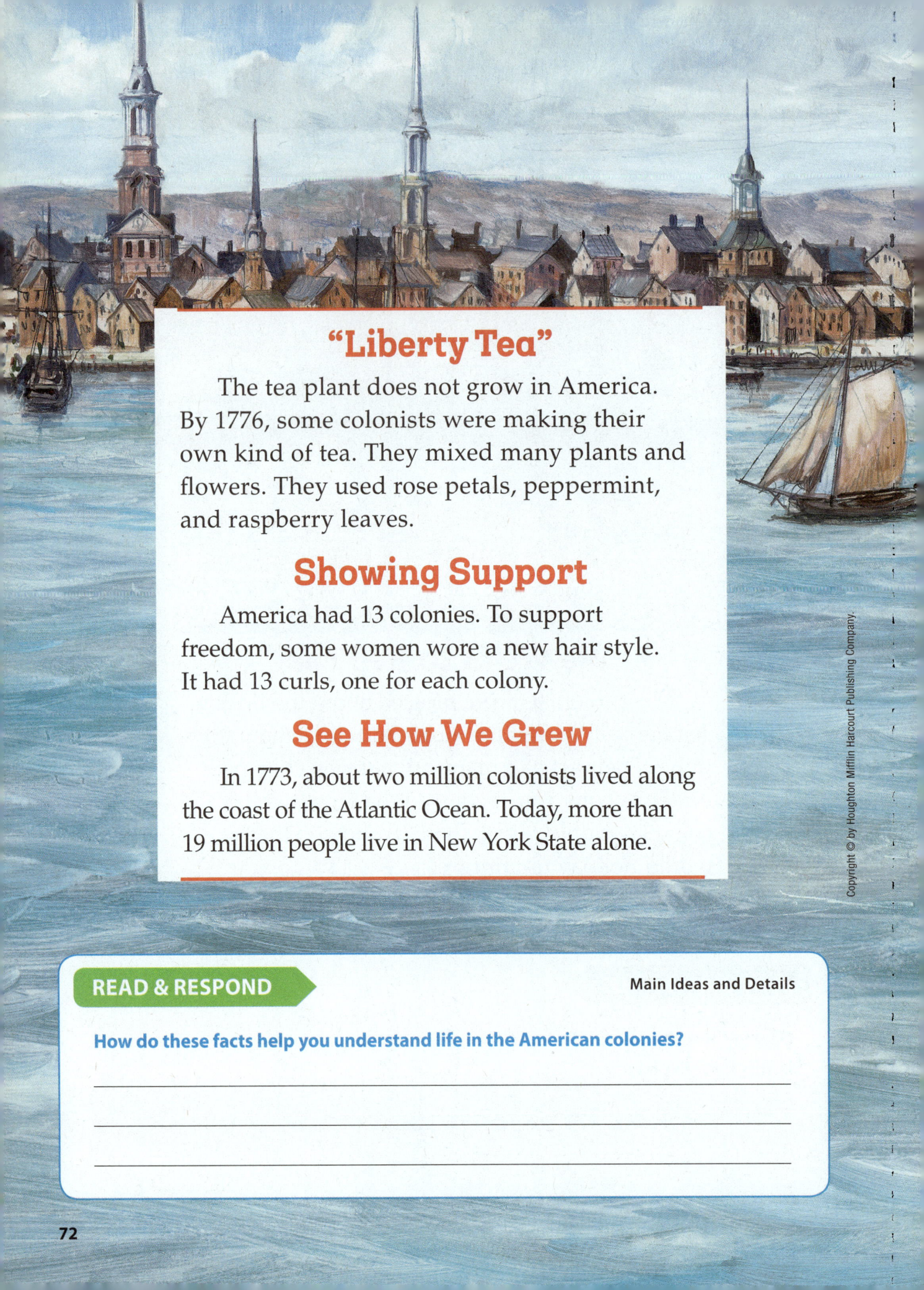

The tea plant does not grow in America. By 1776, some colonists were making their own kind of tea. They mixed many plants and flowers. They used rose petals, peppermint, and raspberry leaves.

Showing Support

America had 13 colonies. To support freedom, some women wore a new hair style. It had 13 curls, one for each colony.

See How We Grew

In 1773, about two million colonists lived along the coast of the Atlantic Ocean. Today, more than 19 million people live in New York State alone.

READ & RESPOND Main Ideas and Details

How do these facts help you understand life in the American colonies?

_____
_____
_____

Reread and Respond

1 What was the colonists' opinion of the king's actions?

_____
_____
_____

> **Hint**
> For a clue, see page 66.

2 Which facts tell you how the king punished the colonists?

_____
_____
_____

> **Hint**
> For clues, see page 70.

3 The Boston Tea Party was the bravest thing the Americans had done. Is this sentence a fact or an opinion? Explain.

_____
_____
_____

> **Hint**
> Remember: a fact can be proved, but an opinion cannot.

4 How could the British have supported their opinion that the colonists should pay taxes?

_____
_____
_____

> **Hint**
> Think about what governments use taxes for.

Bison Come Back to the Plains

by Joe Brennan

Kings of the Plains

The Great Plains lie in the middle of the United States. They run all the way from the north to the south. These broad, flat lands have few trees. The plains used to be covered with tall grass that would sway in the wind, and people said they looked like oceans of grass.

Until about 150 years ago, bison were the kings of the plains. More than 30 million of these huge animals roamed there. Today, the United States is home to just 80 thousand bison.

READ & RESPOND

Central Idea

Why did people say the Great Plains looked like "oceans of grass"?

_____
_____
_____

In the days before European settlers arrived, vast herds of bison grazed on the grass of the plains. After they finished grazing in one area, they would move to another location. Herds moved up to four hundred miles south in the winter, and then back north in the spring. They kept moving in search of available fresh grass.

Each year, the bison walked along the same paths. Often they went in a single line. Over time, the bisons' steps wore down the soil. Some paths were worn three feet deep!

READ & RESPOND

Central Idea

Why did the bison have to move from place to place?

_____
_____
_____

Hunting Bison

American Indian tribes shared the Great Plains with the bison. Bison were very important to the Plains Indians. They depended on these animals for food, clothing, and shelter.

The bison were not easy to kill. They weighed over 1,000 pounds. They could run as fast as horses. Their hooves and horns were very sharp. Bison used their broad heads to ram their enemies. The Plains Indians had to find ways to kill the dangerous animals without getting hurt themselves.

READ & RESPOND

Central Idea

Why was hunting bison difficult for Plains Indians?

_____
_____
_____

Before the Plains Indians had horses, hunting was difficult. Hunters would sometimes drive a group of bison along a prepared path. The end of the path was a cliff that would be unobserved by the bison. They would fall over the edge and die. The Plains Indians could then feed their people. Driving bison, however, was not as easy as it sounds. As people say, you can't drive a bison anywhere it doesn't want to go!

After horses came to America, Plains Indians could hunt on horseback with bows and arrows. They killed only the few bison they needed.

> **READ & RESPOND**
>
> **Central Idea**
>
> **Describe the different ways Plains Indians hunted bison.**
> _____
> _____
> _____

Wasting Nothing

The Plains Indians used every part of the animals they hunted. They dried the meat so that it would last for many weeks without spoiling. Bison skins made warm fur coats and blankets. Plains Indians also stretched the skins over frames made of wooden poles. These tepees provided dry, warm homes and were easy to move from one place to another.

The bones of the bison were used to make tools. Chips of dried bison dung were used as fuel for campfires. The Plains Indians made strong leather from bison skins. They used parts of the animals to make boats and bags.

READ & RESPOND

Central Idea

Write three details that tell how American Indians used different parts of the bison.

_____
_____
_____

What Happened to the Bison?

When settlers from Europe arrived in the Great Plains, the days of the huge herds were numbered. The settlers killed bison for sport, and they killed them to clear the path for railways. By the 1880s, fewer than one thousand bison were left in all of North America.

Some men and women saved a group of bison that were left. They brought them to a protected area. More bison were raised from that group. Slowly, the number of bison grew.

The government passed laws protecting bison. National parks were created where bison would be cared for and protected. With our help, bison will always have an open place to eat grass and roam free.

READ & RESPOND

Central Idea

Write two details that describe people's efforts to save bison.

_____
_____
_____

Bison Facts

Most bison are dark brown or black. Every once in a while, a white bison is born. Plains Indians thought white bison were very special. They told many stories of the rare white beasts.

Bison can be over six feet tall and ten to twelve feet long. Male bison are called bulls. They are usually bigger than female bison.

Bison can't see very well. However, they have a keen sense of smell and hearing. They are good at detecting danger from far away. If they hear or smell a ferocious predator, such as a bear, they can get out of harm's way.

READ & RESPOND

Central Idea

How do bison use their senses?

_____
_____
_____

Reread and Respond

1 **What is this text mainly about? How can you tell?**

_____

_____

_____

> **Hint**
> What are most of the section heads about?

2 **Why were bison paths three feet lower than the ground on either side?**

_____

_____

_____

> **Hint**
> For a clue, see page 75.

3 **Why did bison almost disappear from Earth?**

_____

_____

_____

> **Hint**
> Look for clues on page 79.

4 **Predict what will happen to bison in the future. Use details from the text to support your answer.**

_____

_____

_____

> **Hint**
> For a clue, see page 79.

MODULE 4 WEEK 2

Nero Hawley's Dream
by Joe Brennan

The American Revolution had started. All over the country, Patriots were fighting for freedom. The British were fighting back.

At first, not everyone was allowed to join the Patriot cause. Many Patriot leaders didn't want to allow free or enslaved African American men to take part. Then the British offered freedom to any enslaved man who would join their side.

READ & RESPOND

Central Idea

Reread the title. Do you think it is a clue that tells what this text will be mostly about? Explain.

_____

_____

This worried the Patriots. They needed more men. So they allowed free African American men to join up. Some white men who didn't want to go to war sent slaves in their place as well.

Nero Hawley was one of those enslaved men. He had worked in a sawmill in Connecticut. In the fall of 1777, his master sent him to join the army.

READ & RESPOND

Monitor and Clarify

Do you understand why Nero Hawley was sent to war? Explain.

_____
_____
_____

83

The Patriots promised to free any slaves who fought on their side. Throughout the war, Hawley held on to this promise of freedom. He looked forward to the day he would no longer be enslaved.

Some aspects of army life were new to Hawley. As a soldier, he was paid a small amount each month. Before, he hadn't been paid. He ate and worked with other soldiers, black and white. Before, he had only worked with other enslaved people.

READ & RESPOND

Central Idea

How do the details on this page connect to the central idea?

_____
_____
_____

Hawley was sent to Pennsylvania. There he joined General George Washington's troops. Washington was one of the most influential leaders in the war. He commanded a huge army of soldiers.

Washington ordered his troops to set up camp at Valley Forge. As the army made camp, snow began to fall. It kept falling. The soldiers knew that the coming winter would be long and hard.

READ & RESPOND

Central Idea

Why does the author include details about George Washington? Are they important to the central idea? Explain.

_____

_____

The winter at Valley Forge was even harder than the soldiers had expected. Hawley shared a hut with twelve other soldiers. The snow fell and then melted. Then more snow fell. It melted. The men couldn't keep dry. The army had begun to run out of provisions. There was hardly any food or clothing. Many soldiers had no shoes, and the huts were freezing.

READ & RESPOND

Central Idea

What details show how hard life was for soldiers in the American Revolution? Use the illustrations to help you.

_____
_____

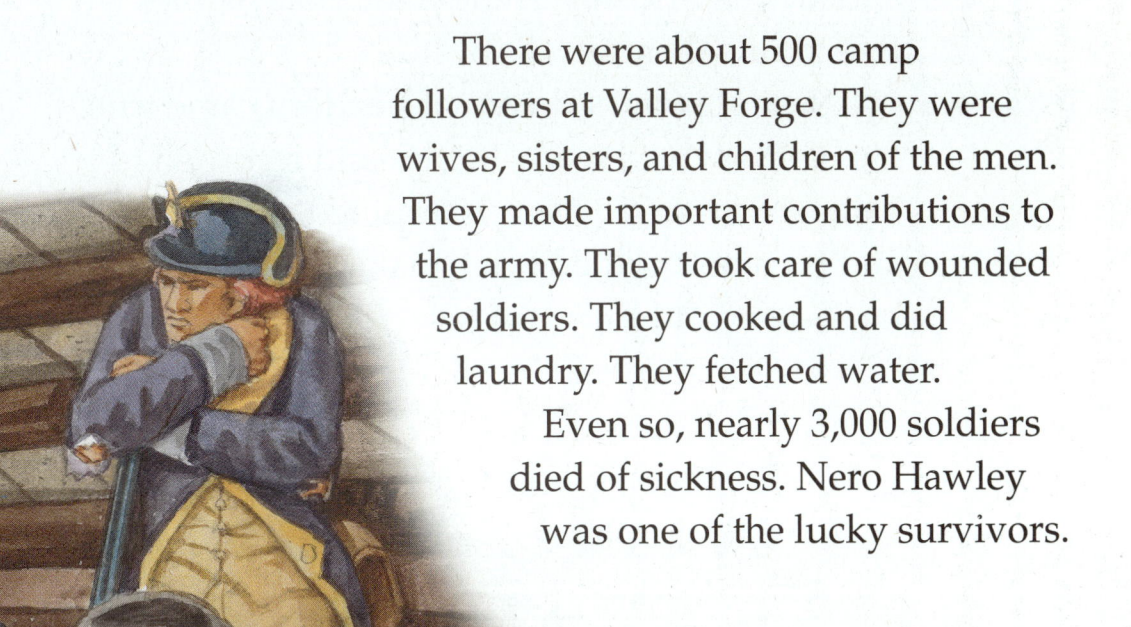

There were about 500 camp followers at Valley Forge. They were wives, sisters, and children of the men. They made important contributions to the army. They took care of wounded soldiers. They cooked and did laundry. They fetched water.

Even so, nearly 3,000 soldiers died of sickness. Nero Hawley was one of the lucky survivors.

READ & RESPOND

Monitor and Clarify

Use what you know to understand why the camp followers' help was important. Explain.

_____
_____

In October 1781, the long, terrible war finally ended. The British surrendered. The colonies were free to rule themselves.

Nero Hawley's dream of freedom came true. He had survived many battles and returned to Connecticut a free man. He trained as an apprentice and became a skilled brick maker. Hawley lived to be 75 years old.

READ & RESPOND

Central Idea

What was Nero Hawley's dream?

_____
_____
_____

Reread and Respond

1 Who was in charge of the army that Nero Hawley joined?

_____

_____

_____

> **Hint**
> For a clue, see page 85.

2 What happened to Nero Hawley after he came home from the war?

_____

_____

_____

> **Hint**
> For a clue, see page 88.

3 What caused so many deaths at Valley Forge?

_____

_____

_____

> **Hint**
> For clues, see pages 86 and 87.

4 Write these events of Hawley's life in order: he works as a brick maker; he camps at Valley Forge; he works in a sawmill; he joins Washington's army.

_____

_____

_____

> **Hint**
> For clues, look through the story.

MODULE 4 WEEK 3

Horse Rider

by Judy Rosenbaum

The bus ride had already lasted an hour. No wonder the people at the Community Center had asked Celia Rivera and her mother to travel with Mrs. Grant and her granddaughter, Daisy. The Grants were new in Williston. They never would have found the Sunflower Stables on their own.

As Celia's mom chatted with Mrs. Grant, Daisy just stared out the window. Daisy's nervous expression made Celia wonder if that girl ever went outside at all. Mom had explained that Mrs. Grant was homeschooling Daisy for now. "Daisy is still feeling the effects of a very bad event," Mom had told Celia. "We hope that the people at Sunflower Stables can help make her feel better."

Celia was glad that she and Mom could also help, even if it was just a little bit.

READ & RESPOND

Point of View

What pronouns do you see on this page? How do they help you know who is telling the story?

_____
_____

The bus stopped at last. The Riveras and the Grants descended the steps. Mom checked her map to see where they had to walk. After ten minutes, they reached the stables.

Inside the grounds were several fenced-in rings. In one, a woman was leading a horse with a boy riding it. A man walked alongside. He held onto the boy. Celia's eyes widened. Wow, horses were huge! The boy looked happy. Outside the ring stood an empty wheelchair.

Mom had explained that spending time on horseback often helped people with some kinds of disabilities. But how could a large animal help a scared kid like Daisy?

READ & RESPOND

Visualize

Does the photo match the picture that the words on this page paint in your mind? Explain.

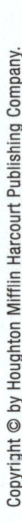

Daisy didn't have a physical challenge. Mentally, however, she had not yet recovered from a tornado in her old town. She had been trapped in the ruins of a shopping mall for hours. Daisy still had nightmares. Even now, she almost never spoke. The family had moved from their old town to Williston. But nothing had helped Daisy.

A woman came over to them. She said, "Hello, Daisy. I'm your side walker, Margie. When you're riding on your horse, I'll hold onto you."

Daisy didn't say a word. A man led a horse out of the barn, and Daisy's hand quivered as she reached for her grandmother. Even Celia backed up when the large, large horse got close.

READ & RESPOND

Main Ideas and Details

What is the main problem described on this page?

_____
_____
_____

"This is Rudy," said Margie, introducing the man. "He's one of our riding teachers." The man smiled and shook hands with Mom and Mrs. Grant.

"And this is Comet," said the man, introducing the horse. "She's an eight-year-old mare."

Comet's large, brown head seemed to loom over Celia. The horse's eyes were huge. Her mouth was huge. Her teeth were probably huge, too. Her neck and chest seemed to be made of muscles. Celia was sure that at any moment, the horse would rear up on her back legs. Then she would be ten feet tall—at least! "Oh, why did I have to think of that?" Celia said to herself.

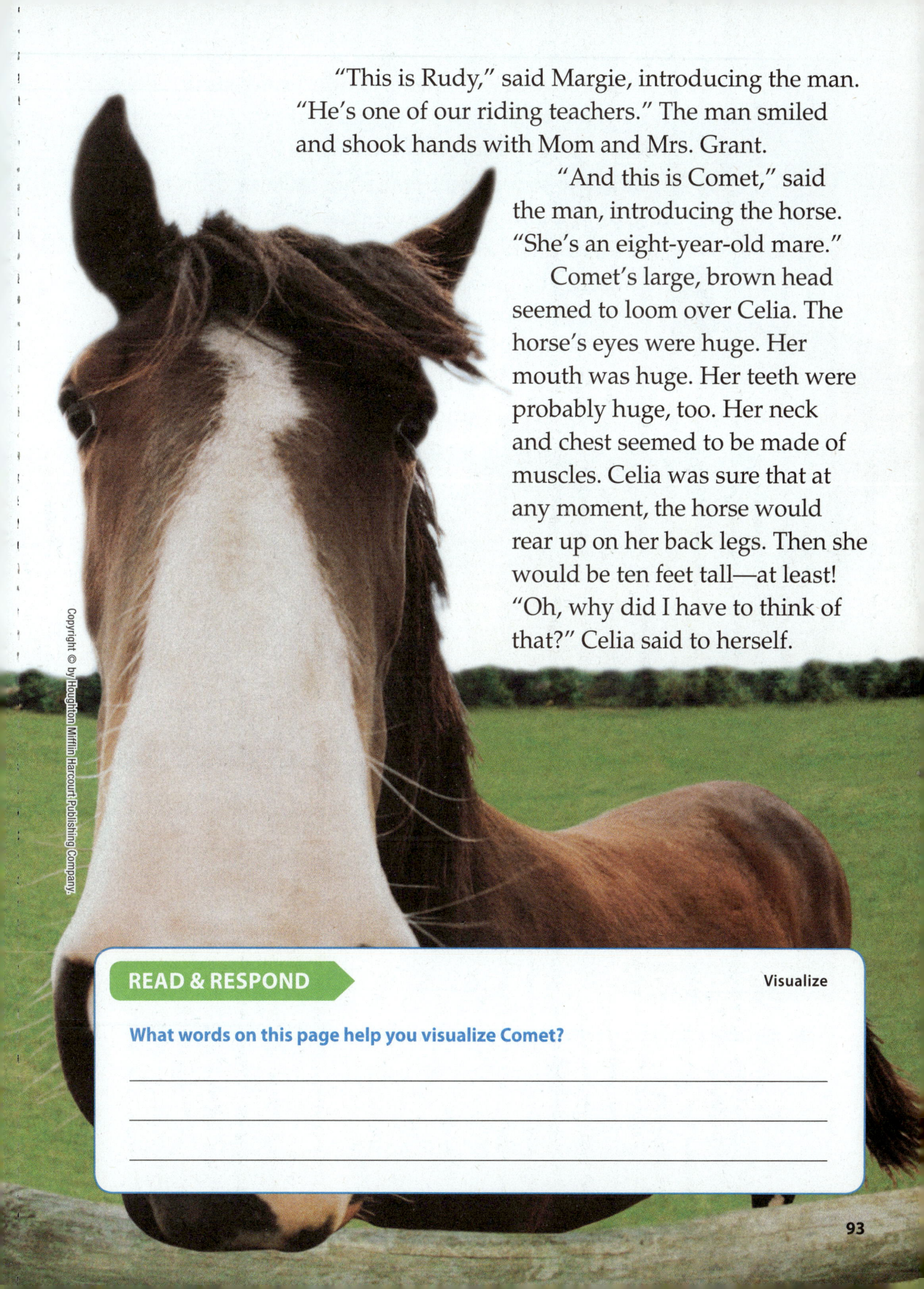

READ & RESPOND

Visualize

What words on this page help you visualize Comet?

_____
_____
_____

"Don't worry, Comet is gentle," said Rudy. "Look how velvety her nose is. Would you like to touch it, Daisy?" Rudy held Comet's head steady and showed Daisy how to touch a horse's nose. Daisy didn't say anything, but to Celia's surprise, Daisy did reach out cautiously and stroke the bridge of that big nose. Celia found herself reaching for Comet's nose, too. It did feel like velvet. She felt her own fear diminishing.

Then Rudy showed how smoothly the horse walked. Comet's hooves made a rhythmic sound on the hard earth.

Margie turned to Celia and said, "How would you like to show Daisy how to sit on a horse?"

READ & RESPOND

Point of View

Is the narrator a character in the story or outside of the story? How do you know?

_____
_____
_____

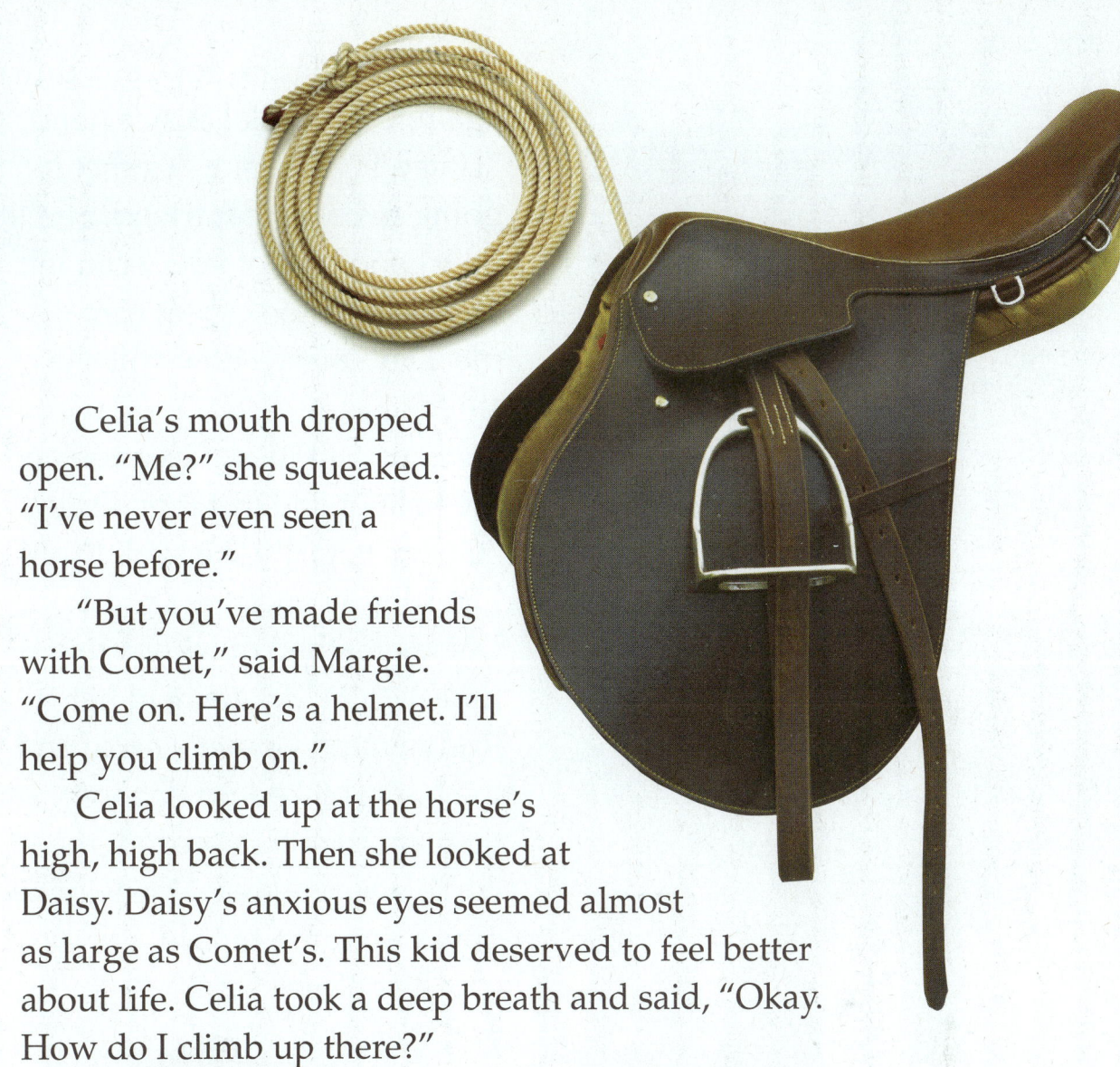

Celia's mouth dropped open. "Me?" she squeaked. "I've never even seen a horse before."

"But you've made friends with Comet," said Margie. "Come on. Here's a helmet. I'll help you climb on."

Celia looked up at the horse's high, high back. Then she looked at Daisy. Daisy's anxious eyes seemed almost as large as Comet's. This kid deserved to feel better about life. Celia took a deep breath and said, "Okay. How do I climb up there?"

With a lot of help from Rudy, Celia still wasn't exactly sure how she ended up on Comet's back. To her surprise, the saddle was pretty comfortable. She looked down, marveling at how still the horse was. "Hey, Daisy, it's fun up here!" she said. It was fun.

READ & RESPOND

Visualize

What details on this page help you visualize Celia and Daisy?

_____
_____
_____

When Margie got Celia down again, Celia took Daisy's hand. "Daisy," Celia said, "Comet is going to be a great friend. She'll take good care of you. I can tell because she took great care of me. Did you see how still she stood?"

Daisy nodded. Celia took off the helmet and put it on Daisy. "Go for it, girl!" she said. Rudy lifted Daisy onto the saddle. Daisy breathed quickly a few times while Margie held her. Rudy patted Comet's neck, and the horse picked up one foot, and then another. In a second, the horse was walking. Daisy looked down from the saddle.

"Cool!" she said.

READ & RESPOND

Point of View

Rewrite the last paragraph from Daisy's point of view.

_____
_____
_____

96

Reread and Respond

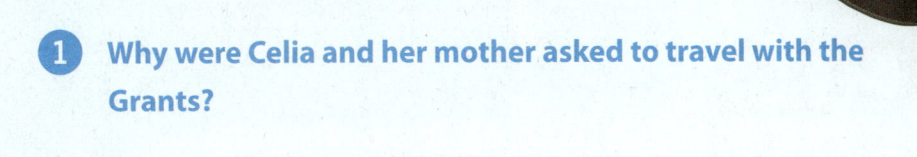

1 Why were Celia and her mother asked to travel with the Grants?

_____
_____
_____

Hint
For clues, see page 90.

2 What problem almost gets in the way of Celia's being able to help Daisy?

_____
_____
_____

Hint
For clues, see pages 91, 93, and 95.

3 What effect does Celia's brave act have on Daisy?

_____
_____
_____

Hint
For clues, see pages 95 and 96.

4 Do you think the author believes that animals can help people feel better? Use details from the story to support your answer.

_____
_____
_____

Hint
You can find clues on almost every page.

MODULE 5 WEEK 1

The Rescue Helicopter Team

by Laurie Rozakis

Ready for Rescue

It seemed like a perfect day, so the rescue helicopter team didn't expect to be very busy. The team did almost all of its work in bad weather. That was when people most needed help.

Then the weather started to change. The sky turned dark, and the wind picked up. A storm was blowing in.

A voice came over the radio. The team was told that it was critical to get ready. The storm was going to hit hard, and soon.

READ & RESPOND Main Ideas and Details

Why does the helicopter rescue team do most of its work in bad weather?

_____
_____
_____

Trouble at Sea

Out on the ocean, Manny and Elena had been enjoying a pleasant day of sailing. They hadn't been prepared for the storm that rushed in.

Suddenly clouds covered the sun. The air became clammy and cold. The wind howled, and waves pounded the little boat.

Manny tried his best to control the boat, but the storm was too strong. The sails ripped and the mast was demolished. Elena rushed into the cabin and sent a distress call over the radio.

READ & RESPOND

Author's Craft

Give at least two examples of vivid, descriptive words found on this page.

_____
_____
_____

Rescue at Sea

Elena's call reached the rescue center. The controller found out what the situation was. He quickly alerted the rescue helicopter team and gave them details of the emergency.

The team raced to their helicopter. They started the engines. It was going to be a busy day after all.

READ & RESPOND　　　　　　　　　　Main Ideas and Details

Why does the team race to its helicopter?

_____
_____
_____

The helicopter arrived at the damaged boat in no time. Its crew lowered a basket to the deck. One of the crew went with it. He had to shout his instructions to be heard over all of the commotion. He helped Elena into the basket.

The basket was quickly pulled back up. Elena was safe in the helicopter. Then the basket was lowered again to rescue Manny.

READ & RESPOND

Author's Craft

How does the author show that the storm and helicopter are loud?

The wind continued to howl. The sea continued to crash. The pilot kept the helicopter still, above the little boat. The rescue crew stayed calm.

Manny struggled into the basket and was carried up into the helicopter. It wouldn't be long before a team member would bundle him up in a dry blanket. Soon after that, he and Elena would be safe back on land.

READ & RESPOND

Author's Craft

Reread this sentence: "It wouldn't be long before a team member would bundle him up in a dry blanket." Why do you think the author included this detail?

_____
_____

Another Emergency

The rescue team's work was not over for the day. The controller had another emergency for the team to handle.

The storm had hit hard on land, too. Up in the mountains, a car had skidded out of control. It had crashed into a tree, and the driver was badly hurt. An ambulance would take a while to reach the accident, but there was no time to waste. The rescue helicopter was up in the air again. There was a doctor on board.

READ & RESPOND

Author's Craft

What mood does the author create by using the words "skidded" and "crashed"?

___

103

Rescue on Land

Ten minutes later, the helicopter reached the scene. It landed at the side of the highway, and the team ran out to the injured driver. He was quickly lifted onto a stretcher and flown right to the hospital. The pilot landed on the helicopter pad on the hospital roof.

It was all in a day's work for the rescue helicopter team.

READ & RESPOND

Main Ideas and Details

What details show that the helicopter team works fast?

_____
_____
_____

Reread and Respond

1 **Would working on a rescue helicopter team be dangerous? Explain.**

_____

_____

_____

Hint
For clues, see pages 101 and 102.

2 **Why are rescue helicopters needed?**

_____

_____

_____

Hint
There are clues throughout the story.

3 **Why might a hospital have a helicopter pad on the roof, instead of on the ground?**

_____

_____

_____

Hint
For a clue, think about a hospital that you have seen.

4 **In what ways can bad weather cause disasters?**

_____

_____

_____

Hint
For clues, see pages 99 and 103.

MODULE 5
WEEK 2

Oil Spill in Alaska

by Richard Stull

My name is Kim. My family and I live in a small town. The town is on the coast of Alaska.

One day after breakfast, my mom and I waved goodbye to my dad. He was heading out to sea on his boat. My dad is a fisherman. As we looked at the ocean, we did not know that something terrible was about to happen.

READ & RESPOND

Literary Elements

What setting is introduced on this page?

_____
_____
_____

Mom heard the news on the radio. An oil tanker had drifted too close to shore. Rocks in the shallow water had ripped a hole in the bottom of the tanker. Thousands of gallons of oil were spilling into the ocean.

My dad's boat returned early that afternoon. I ran to the dock to meet him. "The oil has spread for miles," he said. It had covered birds and sea animals. The oil was also being carried ashore by waves. As a result, vegetation along the coast was covered with oil.

READ & RESPOND

Synthesize

Write one thing you already know about oil spills or one thing you would like to know about oil spills.

_____
_____

A group of men and women met at the mayor's office. They wanted to learn more about the oil spill. The mayor told them that government workers were on their way to start cleaning the oil.

Some of the people wanted to help. "It's our duty as citizens to help clean this oil spill," said my mother.

"I agree," said the mayor. "We all live and work here. We should help clean up this mess."

READ & RESPOND

Literary Elements

Why did a group of the town's citizens meet with the mayor?

_____
_____
_____

High school students also wanted to help. They agreed with my mother and the mayor. The students also felt that humans had a responsibility to help the wild animals.

"Humans made this mess," one student pointed out. "That is why we owe it to the animals to help them."

Everyone decided that they should help clean up the oil spill.

READ & RESPOND

Synthesize

What is one thing you have learned about oil spills while reading this text?

_____
_____
_____

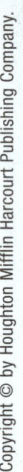

For weeks, everyone worked hard at the cleanup. People cleaned the beaches. They tried to clean as much oil from plants as they could.

They cleaned birds and other animals. Some were soaked with oil. They gave special care to endangered animals. These are animals in danger of dying out completely. My dad explained to me that the Eskimo curlew, a bird that lives along the shore, is one such animal.

READ & RESPOND

Literary Elements

Why were people cleaning beaches?

_____
_____
_____

One day, a woman who worked for the government spoke to us. She said that the efforts to restore the ocean and shore were ending. "Most of the oil has been removed," she said. She then said that things would be much better in a year or two.

My dad was soon able to fish again. I could play on the beach again. During the cleanup, I hadn't been allowed near the water.

READ & RESPOND

Literary Elements

What happened after the cleanup ended?

_____
_____
_____

The oil spill taught all of us valuable lessons. We learned that human actions can have both bad and good effects. Humans caused the oil spill. People working together cleaned it up.

Maybe the oil companies learned a lesson, too. They should know that they must regulate their shipping more carefully. This will help prevent oil spills. Preventing oil spills helps to protect animals and plants on Earth.

READ & RESPOND

Synthesize

Did reading this text change your mind about the oil industry? Explain.

_____
_____
_____

Reread and Respond

1 What effects does the oil spill have on the environment?
_____
_____
_____

> **Hint**
> For clues, see pages 107, 110, and 111.

2 How does the oil spill affect the people of the town?
_____
_____
_____

> **Hint**
> You can find clues on almost every page.

3 Do you think the people succeeded in cleaning up the oil spill?
_____
_____
_____

> **Hint**
> For clues, see pages 110 and 111.

4 What point does the author make about taking responsibility?
_____
_____
_____

> **Hint**
> You can find clues on pages 108, 109, and 112.

MODULE 5 WEEK 3

The Long Flight

by Mia Lewis

The Monarch's Migration

It is late August on the border of Canada and the United States. A gorgeous monarch butterfly has just struggled out of its chrysalis. This butterfly is different from its parents and grandparents. It will not lay eggs right away like most females. It will live much longer than the monarchs that were born earlier in the summer.

This butterfly will make an amazing journey. So will millions just like it. They will make their way to winter homes in Mexico and southern California.

READ & RESPOND

Text and Graphic Features

How does the illustration help you know what a monarch butterfly looks like?

_____
_____
_____

The monarch will fly high. It may fly almost two miles up in the sky. Its wings will beat from five to twelve times every second. It will fly thousands of miles to a place it has never seen.

Soon millions of monarchs will be in the air. A monarch usually lives alone. Now it travels with a large group of other monarchs. They will sip nectar from flowers along the way. This gives them the energy they need for the long trip.

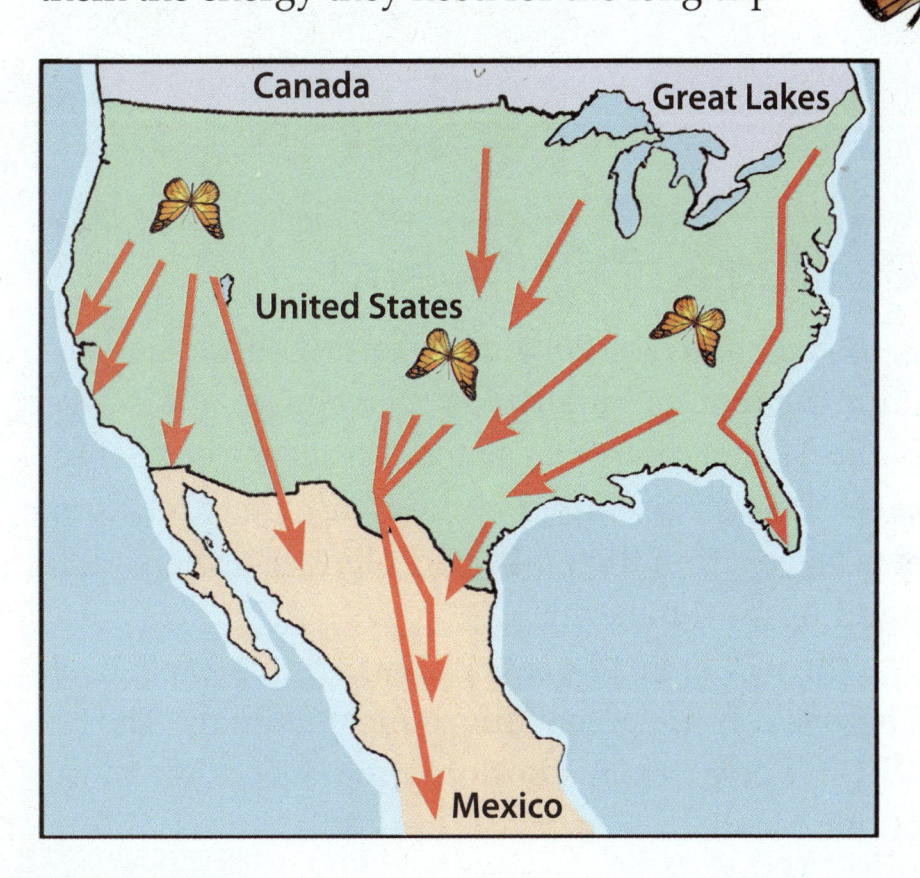

READ & RESPOND

Text and Graphic Features

Look at the map. What is the destination for butterflies that start out near the Great Lakes?

_____
_____

Egg

Larva (caterpillar)

Life Stages of the Monarch

All monarch butterflies go through four stages. First, the mother butterfly lays an egg on a milkweed plant. Then a caterpillar hatches from the egg. The caterpillar is very hungry. It eats the egg case. Then it eats leaves from the milkweed plant. This helps it to build up fat for energy.

The monarch also eats milkweed to protect itself. These leaves are poisonous to most animals. They will stay away from a butterfly that has eaten a lot of this plant!

READ & RESPOND

Text and Graphic Features

Look at the diagram on this page. What are two names for the second stage in the monarch's life?

_____

_____

Chrysalis

Adult (butterfly)

The caterpillar makes a chrysalis. Inside, it gradually changes. Finally, a butterfly crawls out! It rests. It waits for its wings to dry. When they are dry, the monarch will be able to fly. All monarchs are orange and black. They all look very similar. But they are not identical.

Shorter days and cooler weather tell the monarch it is time to leave. It sets off on its long flight. Scientists do not know how it can tell where to go. They think it might use the position of the sun to help it figure out which direction to go.

READ & RESPOND

Text and Graphic Features

Write the stages of a monarch's life in order. Use clues from the text to help you.

_____
_____
_____

Flying South

The distance to the monarch's winter grounds can be as long as three thousand miles. Wind or weather can take the butterfly out of its way, too. The monarch stops flying if the wind is too strong. It stops if it is raining or too hot. The journey takes about two months.

When the monarch finally arrives, there will be millions of other butterflies there. Each year the monarchs return to the same exact trees.

READ & RESPOND

Main Ideas and Details

Why would a monarch stop flying if the wind is strong?

_____
_____
_____

Flying Back Home

Thousands of monarchs crowd together through the winter. They huddle together on the branches to keep warm. Spring finally arrives. The monarch gets ready for the journey home. It will not make it all the way back, though. It will die along the way.

The monarch lays eggs before it dies. These eggs will hatch. The offspring will go through all the same stages and become butterflies. Then they will continue the long trip back to their summer home.

READ & RESPOND	Text and Graphic Features

What does the picture on this page show?

_____

_____

_____

Monarchs in Danger

The pattern will begin again. Summer will come and go. Several sets of monarchs will live their lives. Then autumn will draw near. The last monarchs of summer will get ready for their trip.

Today, monarchs face new dangers. Human activities are disturbing their way of life. There aren't enough safe places left for them anymore. Even their winter resting spots are in danger because trees there are being cut down. Scientists want to protect forests in these areas. That will help the butterflies.

READ & RESPOND

Main Ideas and Details

What is one way that humans are disturbing the monarchs' way of life?

_____
_____
_____

Reread and Respond

1 What is special about the last monarch butterflies to be born each summer?

_____
_____
_____

> **Hint**
> For clues, see page 114.

2 How high can a monarch butterfly fly?

_____
_____
_____

> **Hint**
> For a clue, see page 115.

3 What does the map on page 255 tell you about where in the United States you can find monarch butterflies in the summer?

_____
_____
_____

> **Hint**
> In what parts of the country do the arrows begin?

4 What is so amazing about the monarch's journey to its winter resting place?

_____
_____
_____

> **Hint**
> For clues, see pages 115 and 118.

121

MODULE 6 WEEK 1
On the Beckwourth Trail

by Richard Stull

James Beckwourth stood looking out over the land. Before him lay the Sierra Nevada Mountains. California lay on the other side. His job was to lead a wagon train through the mountains.

The year was 1851. The travelers were part of the California Gold Rush. They all hoped to find gold and become rich. They had hired James to guide them.

James knew the way. In fact, he had discovered the trail through the mountains. James also knew that the travelers undoubtedly needed a guide. Without one, they were sure to get lost.

READ & RESPOND

Make Inferences

Why would travelers get lost without a guide?

_____
_____
_____

That night, James met with the men and women of the wagon train. He first showed them a map he had drawn. "We must keep a steady pace on our trip," he said. "Doing so will help us cross the mountains before the first snows hit."

"What other things should we do on the trip?" asked one man. James told them to avoid wild animals such as bears. He told them to keep the children close to the wagons at all times. He also told them not to waste their drinking water. It was evident to the travelers that James was an experienced mountain man.

READ & RESPOND

Make Inferences

Why does James show a map to the travelers?

_____
_____
_____

123

The trip proved to be difficult, and the days turned into weeks. The travelers knew that the weather would be a huge factor in the success of the journey. They also knew that the first snow would soon fall. Even James began to worry. He decided to have another meeting with the travelers.

"I need to ride ahead," James said. "I will be able to tell how many days we have left before we leave the mountains."

The people looked at one another. They were not sure that they could trust James to return for them. They decided to vote on if he should go or stay.

READ & RESPOND

Make Inferences

Why would the weather be important in the success of the journey?

___
___
___

The travelers decided to let James ride ahead. The next morning, he mounted his horse and rode off. Before he left, he urged the people to keep moving as fast as possible. He told them that he would be back within a week.

The wagon train plodded along. The September nights grew colder and colder. Five days after James left, a woman thought she saw him in the distance. "James has returned," she yelled. As the wagons rolled closer, the people saw that it was an American Indian chief, watching them from afar.

READ & RESPOND

Author's Craft

What is the mood on this page? How does the author create this mood?

_____
_____
_____

125

On the night of the seventh day, the people gathered around their campfires. They were worried that James might not return. They were also worried about the American Indian they had seen. Maybe he was not friendly. Maybe he would return with other warriors.

Suddenly, they heard the sound of a horse traveling fast over the land. Everyone stood up to listen. The adults hid the children in the wagons.

Just then, James rode into the light of the campfires. He hopped down from his horse. "I'm starving," he said. "What's for dinner?"

> **READ & RESPOND**
>
> Author's Craft
>
> How does the author break the suspense he created on this page?
> _____
> _____
> _____

The men and women crowded around James. "How close are we to Marysville?" asked one woman. Marysville was an important and growing city. It was located right in the middle of the area where people were finding gold.

"We're about a week's journey away," explained James. "We're a lot closer than I thought we were."

The people shouted with joy. They knew that they had made it through the mountains in time. They also knew that their brave guide James Beckwourth had been their salvation.

READ & RESPOND

Author's Craft

How do you feel at the end of the story? How does the author make you feel that way?

_____
_____

California Gold Rush
Thousands of people used the Beckwourth Trail during the Gold Rush. The Gold Rush began in 1848 and lasted about 10 years.

The Beckwourth Trail
James opened his wagon trail in 1851. People used the trail to cross the mountains to Marysville.

Marysville, California
The city of Marysville promised to pay James for improving the trail. More people in the city meant more money for everyone. The city did not pay him.

In Thanks
Marysville gave its largest park a new name in 1996. The park is now called Beckwourth Riverfront Park. It honors James Beckwourth.

READ & RESPOND

Author's Craft

How does this feature help you better understand this text?

_____
_____
_____

Reread and Respond

1. What is James Beckwourth's role as the wagon train's guide?
___

Hint
For clues, see pages 122 and 123.

2. What important event occurs during the second meeting between James and the travelers?
___

Hint
For clues, see pages 124 and 125.

3. How would you describe James Beckwourth's character?
___

Hint
You can find clues on almost every page.

4. Do you think the people of Marysville, California, realize what they owe to James Beckwourth? What makes you think the way you do?
___

Hint
For clues, see page 128.

MODULE 6 WEEK 2

The Carpenter and the Drummer Boy

by Duncan Searl

John Potter gathered planks for his uncle's new ship. He was only twelve, but he was already a good carpenter. He had personally helped build three ships at his uncle's boatyard in Bristol Harbor, Rhode Island.

Those ships had all been burned. John's uncle was a Patriot, and the British were at war with Patriots. Earlier that year, redcoats had marched into Bristol and set the ships on fire.

John and his uncle were not discouraged. They were building a new ship. When it was finished, they would sail again. Maybe they would fight the redcoats in it!

> **READ & RESPOND**
>
> Author's Craft
>
> **How does the author show how John Potter feels about the British soldiers? Give at least two examples from the text.**
> _____
> _____

Thomas Strand was British. He was a drummer boy with his father's regiment at Newport, Rhode Island. Wherever the soldiers marched, Thomas led the way. A long line of redcoats followed his drum's sharp rat-a-tat-tat-tat.

"Thomas," the British major called one morning. "Assemble the men!" Thomas began a long drumroll. The redcoats rushed to organize themselves into position.

"We're heading to Bristol!" the major said.

READ & RESPOND

Visualize

What words on this page help you visualize this scene?

_____
_____
_____

The march to Bristol was long, hot, and dusty. Thomas did not feel well. Usually, he loved nothing more than drumming a steady marching beat. Today this chore seemed tedious.

In Bristol, John Potter was alone in the boatyard. He saw the British soldiers coming, and tried to run, but it was too late. The redcoats quickly captured him and tied his hands.

The soldiers were efficient. It took them no time to set fire to the new ship. Then they started the march back to Newport, with John as their prisoner.

READ & RESPOND

Author's Craft

Why do you think the author describes how Thomas feels?

_____
_____
_____

The smoke from the burning ship had brought tears to John's eyes. He wouldn't be sailing with his uncle anytime soon. Worse yet, he was a prisoner. What would the British do with him? John started to feel better when he realized that the march would take them right past his home. Maybe he would catch a glimpse of his mother or sister before going to a British prison.

Thomas Strand was feeling worse and worse. As he led the redcoats along the rural road, he became hungry and tired. Gradually his drumming slowed. Then it stopped completely.

READ & RESPOND

Author's Craft

Explain how John feels while marching as a prisoner. How do you know?

_____
_____
_____

As the redcoats approached John's farmhouse, Thomas fainted and fell to the ground. The major sent two of his men to the house to ask for water.

At first, Mrs. Potter and her daughter Eliza were not anxious to help the redcoats. Then they saw the sick drummer boy lying in the road. "He's no older than our John," Eliza said to her mother. They brought some bread and tea out to Thomas.

READ & RESPOND

Author's Craft

How does the author show that Mrs. Potter's and Eliza's feelings about helping the redcoats change?

_____
_____

Of course, it wasn't long before Mrs. Potter spotted her son. "John!" she called, rushing toward him. "Why are you here with the redcoats?"

"I'm their prisoner, Mother," he replied softly.

Mrs. Potter turned angrily to the major. "What do you mean by this, sir? What right do you have to make my son your prisoner?"

"It is the king's order, Madam," the major answered. "Burn the ships at Bristol and take the Patriots prisoner. That is what we were ordered to do."

READ & RESPOND

Visualize

What details help you visualize John and Mrs. Potter during this scene?

_____
_____
_____

John's sister Eliza spoke in a soft voice. "I know the king would be grateful that we helped his drummer. I think he would show his thanks by freeing my brother now."

"I'm not sure about the king," said the major, "but I will release your brother."

John was untied and freed. He and his mother promised to return Thomas to Newport when he felt better.

Later that day, John and Eliza rowed Thomas back to Newport. "When the war is over," said Thomas, "I will come back here. Maybe I can help you build a new ship."

"Maybe you can," said John.

READ & RESPOND

Visualize

Does this illustration match what you visualize as you read? Explain.

_____
_____
_____

Reread and Respond

1 **Why is Thomas Strand a drummer boy for the British?**

_____
_____
_____

> **Hint**
> For a clue, see page 131.

2 **Compare how Mrs. Potter and Eliza act when they find that John is a prisoner.**

_____
_____
_____

> **Hint**
> For clues, see pages 135 and 136.

3 **What does John Potter expect to happen to him, and what actually happens to him?**

_____
_____
_____

> **Hint**
> For clues, see pages 133 and 136.

4 **Why do you think the major decides to free John in the end?**

_____
_____

> **Hint**
> For clues, see pages 135 and 136.

MODULE 6 WEEK 3

Tomás Decides

by Duncan Searl

"Sit down! Eat!" Mrs. Guzman urged. Before he sat down, Mr. Guzman cleared his throat to speak. "I just want to say how proud I am that Tomás is running for president of the student council."

Poor Tomás squirmed in his seat. Why did his father have to make such a big deal about that?

"My son will be a leader," Mr. Guzman said, "and he will change things for the better!"

Tomás hesitated for a moment. "Thanks, Papa," he said, "but my plans are, um, changing. When my friends asked me to run for student council, I agreed. Now I, er, I want to play baseball."

READ & RESPOND

Literary Elements

What two characters are introduced? How do their plans differ?

_____
_____
_____

138

Mr. Guzman's face fell. He seemed shaken by the news. "Play baseball?" he repeated with a sad smile.

Tomás pressed his case. "That's right. The Raiders have a chance to win the championship," he said. "To do it, the team needs me there, a hundred percent!"

"Can't you do both, Tomás?" Mrs. Guzman asked.

"Not really, Mama. To win the student council seat, I have to give two speeches and take part in a debate. I have to make posters and talk to people. That all happens after school. So I'd miss practice sometimes, maybe even games. Besides, the student council never does anything important."

The rest of the meal passed in silence. Tomás kept his eyes on his plate.

READ & RESPOND

Theme

Explain the problem in this story.

_____
_____
_____

The next morning, Tomás got up and went to school. His head felt heavy. The looks on his parents' faces stayed in his mind.

"Hey, Tomás," Gregory called. "I have some ideas for posters we can make for your student council race." He pulled sketches from his backpack.

Tomás scanned the drawings. "These look great," he said. "By the way, Greg, did you ever think about running for student council yourself?"

"Me?" laughed Greg. "No, but you're a natural for the job. People look up to you, Tomás. You could really get things done around here!"

"Later, Greg," said Tomás, taking the sketches. He didn't have the heart to tell his friend about his change of plans.

READ & RESPOND

Literary Elements and Theme

What evidence in this section shows how Tomás feels?

_____
_____
_____

That afternoon, Tomás's class walked to Golden Greens. The class had already been to the senior citizen home twice. The students went there to talk with the seniors, play games, and learn firsthand about the past.

In the rec room, a tall, skinny man beckoned to Tomás. "Hey, Mr. Guzman! Come on over here and sit awhile." It was Mr. Jeffers, a man Tomás had played checkers with last time.

"Hello, Mr. Jeffers," Tomás said.

Mr. Jeffers smiled. "Call me Fastball."

"Why Fastball?" Tomás asked.

"Well, you know I can't walk anymore, but back in the day, I was a fastball pitcher."

"A major leaguer?" Tomás asked hopefully.

READ & RESPOND

Literary Elements

Who is Mr. Jeffers? How does Tomás know him?

_____
_____
_____

141

Mr. Jeffers smiled. "In the 1930s and 1940s, the Negro Leagues were as major a league as any black man could get into. Even so, I struck out batters with the best of them!"

Tomás had never heard of the Negro Leagues. So Mr. Jeffers showed him a photograph.

"In my day," Mr. Jeffers said, "blacks and whites couldn't play on the same teams. That wasn't right, and it wasn't fair, but that's the way it was."

"That's all changed now," said Tomás.

"Sure has," Mr. Jeffers agreed, "but only because some people cared enough to change it. A few good people changed the rules and the laws, and things got better."

Tomás didn't reply. He was thinking hard.

READ & RESPOND

Theme

Why do you think the author includes information about the Negro Leagues?

_____
_____
_____

Mr. Jeffers broke the silence. "Are you a ballplayer, Tomás?"

"Shortstop. Our team could win the championship."

"Looking forward to that, are you?"

Tomás blurted out his feelings. He told Mr. Jeffers about his dilemma.

"Winning ballgames is good," Mr. Jeffers said. "However, improving a situation can make all the difference. I know from experience."

"Thanks, Fastball," Tomás said. "I guess I'll have to decide."

READ & RESPOND

Literary Elements

What happens after Mr. Jeffers asks if Tomás plays baseball?

_____
_____
_____

VOTE

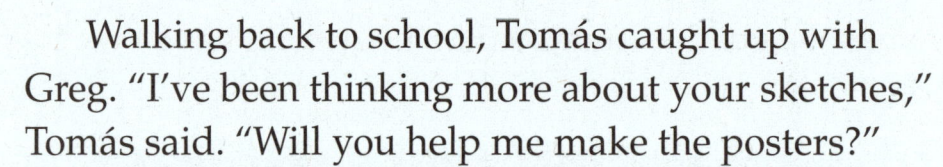

Walking back to school, Tomás caught up with Greg. "I've been thinking more about your sketches," Tomás said. "Will you help me make the posters?"

"Sure," said Greg. "By the way, do you have any ideas for the speech you have to make?"

"We all know our school could be a lot better," said Tomás. "Let's get our friends together after school for a meeting. I want everyone to make some suggestions. We need to choose the ideas that will really make a difference!"

"Don't you have baseball practice?"

"I can go to practice tomorrow," Tomás said. "This is important after all."

READ & RESPOND

Theme

How has Tomás changed?

_____
_____
_____

Reread and Respond

1 **What decision does Tomás have to make?**

_____
_____
_____

> **Hint**
> See pages 138 and 139.

2 **How does Mr. Jeffers help Tomás make his decision?**

_____
_____
_____

> **Hint**
> For a clue, see page 142.

3 **What is the theme of the story?**

_____
_____
_____

> **Hint**
> Think about what Tomás learned or how he changed.

4 **Do you think Tomás makes the right decision? Why?**

_____
_____
_____

> **Hint**
> Your answers to questions 2 and 3 should help you.

The Story of Bunker's Cove

by Mia Lewis

Jack Bunker was an old salt. An old salt is a sailor who has sailed on ships for many years. Jack wasn't old, but he had sailed on many ships!

Jack and his sister Comfort lived in Maine. Jack lived on Cranberry Island, near the coast. Comfort and her husband John lived at Norwood's Cove on a farm near the water. Their home was happy and quiet. They felt no pressing need to become involved with politics.

READ & RESPOND

Ideas and Support

Give examples of one fact and one opinion that appear on this page.

Life in Maine was peaceful. In other parts of New England, though, the colonists were angry with Britain. Colonists had no say in the laws that the British made for them. If they couldn't have representatives, colonial Patriots wanted freedom from the British. The British soldiers sailed to America to stop the Patriots. By 1775, the American Revolution had started.

READ & RESPOND

Ideas and Support

The author says life in Maine was peaceful. Is that a fact or an opinion? Explain.

_____
_____
_____

One day, John and Comfort went to visit friends. While they were gone, a British ship arrived. The British killed the cows on the farm and burned the house. They left a note that said, "Starve!"

Jack was very upset at the conduct of the British soldiers. He decided to do something. He and a friend traveled by canoe for many days until they found a big British boat named the *Falmouth Packet*. It was anchored offshore, full of food and supplies. Its crew was on land.

READ & RESPOND

Make and Confirm Predictions

What do you think Jack and his friend will do to the boat?

_____
_____
_____

Jack and his friend climbed onto the boat and put up the sails. They sailed to Norwood's Cove and gave his sister all the supplies. Then he decided to hide the boat. He didn't want the British to be able to use it to fight the Patriots.

A crew of friends helped Jack sail the boat out to sea. There were many British warships out there. One captain surveyed the sea and saw Jack. He began to chase the slower supply boat. Jack was a fine sailor. He knew how to make the *Falmouth Packet* go fast. Could he go fast enough?

| READ & RESPOND | Make and Confirm Predictions |

Do you think Jack will go fast enough? Explain your prediction.

Jack thought of a special place to hide the boat. He sailed it into a little cove. The British couldn't see where the boat had gone. Then Jack and his friends decided to cut down the masts. The British saw the masts fall. Now they knew where the *Falmouth Packet* was hidden.

READ & RESPOND Ideas and Support

Is this statement a fact or an opinion: "Jack was a fine sailor"?

_____
_____
_____

The British captain didn't want to sail into the little cove at first. His viewpoint was that the rocks would sink the big ship. Finally, he and some of his men took a small rowboat into the cove. They looked around, but they didn't see Jack or the *Falmouth Packet*.

Jack and his friends had taken the *Falmouth Packet* close to the land. They cut a hole in the bottom of the boat. It sank into the mud. Then they covered it with tree branches and seaweed.

READ & RESPOND

Make and Confirm Predictions

Did you predict that Jack and his friends would sink the *Falmouth Packet*? Why, or why not?

_____
_____

Jack and his friends escaped in two rowboats. They rowed at night and hid during the day. After a long journey, they finally arrived home.

These daring men helped the Patriots fight the British. The United States eventually won the war. The colonies were free.

Jack didn't stop sailing. He lived to be a really old salt! Today the little cove where Jack hid the *Falmouth Packet* is named Bunker's Cove.

READ & RESPOND

Ideas and Support

What did the author want readers to learn?

_____
_____
_____

Reread and Respond

1 What did the British soldiers do that made Jack angry?

_____

_____

_____

> **Hint**
> For clues, look on page 148.

2 Why did Jack bring the *Falmouth Packet* to Norwood Cove?

_____

_____

_____

> **Hint**
> For a clue, see page 149.

3 Write three words to describe Jack.

_____

_____

_____

> **Hint**
> You can find clues all through the story.

4 How did Jack and his friends help the Patriots defeat the British?

_____

_____

_____

> **Hint**
> Think what would have happened if Jack had NOT taken the British supply ship.

The Cattle Drive

by Richard Stull

By 1866, most of the beef that was eaten in the East came from Texas. Ranchers in Texas first had to move their cattle to Chicago. That's where the meatpacking plants were. The beef was then packed and shipped by train to eastern cities.

Moving a herd of cattle was called cattle driving. Ranchers hired cowboys to move the cows. About ten or twelve cowboys could move a herd of 3,000 cows.

READ & RESPOND

Central Idea

Does the drawing give clues about the central idea of this text? Explain.

_____
_____
_____

The cattle drives started in Texas. They ended in Sedalia, Missouri, where there was a railroad. From there, the cows were shipped by train to Chicago.

There was one problem. The trail to Missouri went through farms in eastern Kansas. The residents along the trail did not want the cows crossing their land. They thought the cattle carried disease. The cows also trampled and ate the farmers' crops.

READ & RESPOND

Central Idea

Where did cattle drives begin? Where did they end?

_____
_____
_____

Fights broke out between farmers and cowboys. The cowboys did not want to fight the farmers, so they started moving the cows along a different trail.

This new trail did not go through the farms of eastern Kansas. It ended in a town in western Kansas. The town was Abilene. Abilene also had a railroad extending all the way to Chicago.

READ & RESPOND

Central Idea

Why did the cattle drive trail change?

_____
_____
_____

156

A cattle drive was hard work. The trail from Texas to Abilene was about a thousand miles long. The trip could take almost two months. During that time, the cowboys herded the cattle across rivers and small mountain ranges.

During the day, the cowboys drove the herd along the trail. At night, they watched the cattle to guard against thieves and watch for stampedes. The cowboys took turns sleeping and watching.

READ & RESPOND

Central Idea

Give one detail that explains why cattle drives were hard work.

___
___
___

The cowboys drove the cows over the sprawling Indian Territory. The land is now part of Oklahoma. The American Indians there were not hostile. In fact, they made money from cattle drives. The cowboys had to pay the tribes ten cents for each cow that passed through their land.

When they reached the railroad in Abilene, the cowboys sold the herd. They then rode back to Texas.

READ & RESPOND

Central Idea

Why did cowboys drive cattle to Abilene?

_____
_____
_____

The time of the great cattle drives lasted about twenty years. In that time, many people prospered. Ranchers became rich. Railroads made money. The meatpackers made money. Owners of stores in towns such as Abilene made money. Even the cowboys made money.

READ & RESPOND

Central Idea

What is the main idea of this paragraph? How does it connect to the central idea?

_____
_____
_____

By 1890, things had changed. Railroads ran to Texas and other states in the West. Meatpacking plants had been built throughout the West. The ranchers in Texas did not have to drive their cows to Kansas. The cows did not have to be shipped by train to Chicago. The age of the great cattle drives had come to an end.

READ & RESPOND

Central Idea

What is the central idea of this text?

_____
_____
_____

Reread and Respond

1 Why did the ranchers in Texas have to move their cows to Chicago?

_____
_____
_____

> **Hint**
> For clues, see page 154.

2 What details explain why the farmers were not happy about the cows crossing their land?

_____
_____
_____

> **Hint**
> You can find clues on page 155.

3 What graphic source would help to make the cross-country cattle trails more clear for the reader? Explain.

_____
_____
_____

> **Hint**
> Think about a graphic source you use when traveling.

4 Would you have wanted to go on a cattle drive? Explain.

_____
_____
_____

> **Hint**
> Think about what you learned about cattle drives.

MODULE 7 WEEK 3

It Takes Teamwork

by Mia Lewis

Sitting at her desk, Carla scanned the line of classmates as they filed in to take their seats.

"What happened to you?" she asked a dripping Ben as he shuffled into class. His soaked sneakers squeaked as he passed by.

"I was waiting at the bus stop when this huge truck came down the hill and splashed me!" he said.

"Looks like you and the truck started the day on a downhill slope," Carla joked.

READ & RESPOND

Literary Elements

Where does this story take place? How do you know?

_____
_____
_____

162

"This is Teamwork Week," said Ms. Kim. "You will team up with a classmate to make a model of some kind."

Carla decided she would ask Ben. They would make a good team.

"Typically, I let you pick your own partners," explained Ms. Kim. "This time I am going to pull two names at a time from a box. The names I pick will be teammates."

Carla sat completely still as Ms. Kim called out the names.

"Carla Vargas and, let's see, Wendell Oaks."

"Oh, no," Carla said to herself. "I don't know him."

READ & RESPOND

Author's Craft

Explain how including Carla's thoughts helps readers understand more about her personality.

_____

_____

163

Carla agreed to meet Wendell after school to work on the project.

Later, at Wendell's home, Mrs. Oaks greeted Carla and invited her to come inside. "Wendell is down in his lab," she explained.

"Lab? Just what am I getting into now?" Carla wondered as she stepped down the stairs.

In the basement, Wendell had just finished working on a model car.

"Do you like making models?" Carla asked.

"I sure do," Wendell said. "Do you?"

READ & RESPOND

Literary Elements

Explain the setting for this part of the story.

_____
_____
_____

"I'm no good at it," Carla said. She was embarrassed to tell about the model boat she made last year. It had floated for only a few seconds.

"Well, it takes two to make a team," said Wendell. "I'm sure you have a talent to add."

"I *am* good at coming up with ideas and making plans," offered Carla. "What if we make a model for an amusement park ride?"

"Yes!" Wendell agreed. "Let's make it a floating boat ride."

"Um, sure," said Carla, sounding very uncertain.

READ & RESPOND

Literary Elements

What skills does Carla have that she can contribute to the team?

_____
_____
_____

Carla made a preliminary sketch before they began to build. Wendell looked for materials. It was obvious that Wendell knew what he was doing! Carla was amazed at the hanging vines he made out of clay. Carla made a cave for the boat ride.

The teammates put the model in a pan filled with water. The water was a lake around the island. They made small boats from small trays. The trays had little foam balls underneath to help keep them afloat. Wendell linked the boats with string.

READ & RESPOND

Author's Craft

How does the author show that Wendell knows how to make models?

_____
_____
_____

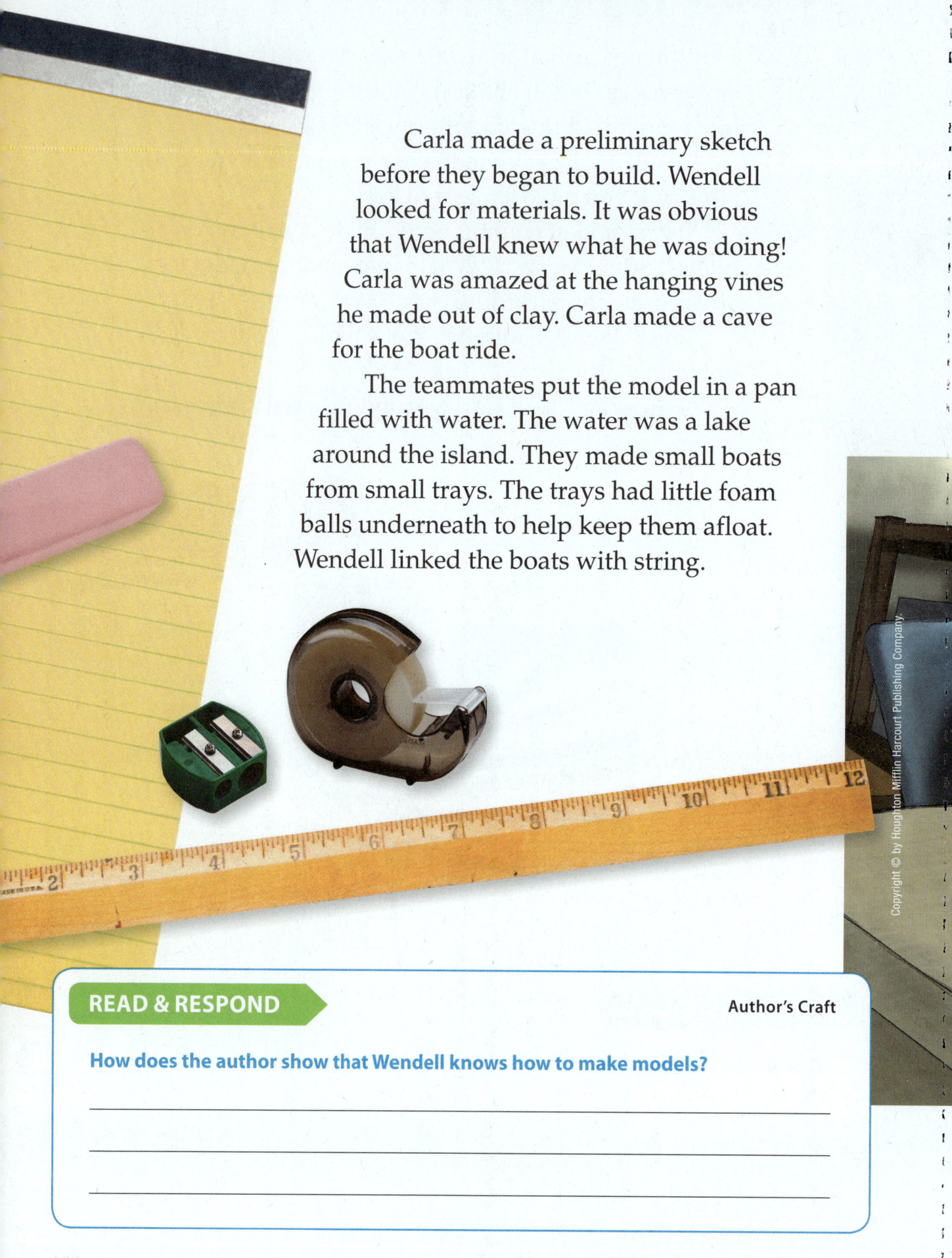

"Wendell is an artist, a brain, and a good teammate," Carla said to herself.

When the model was done, the boats went around the lake and floated in and out of the cave. The whole thing looked gorgeous!

"We did it!" Carla exclaimed as Wendell sat back and admired the model. "Let's make a recording of water burbling, like in a stream," she said. "We can play it while we give our presentation."

"Good plan!" agreed Wendell, reaching for a recorder.

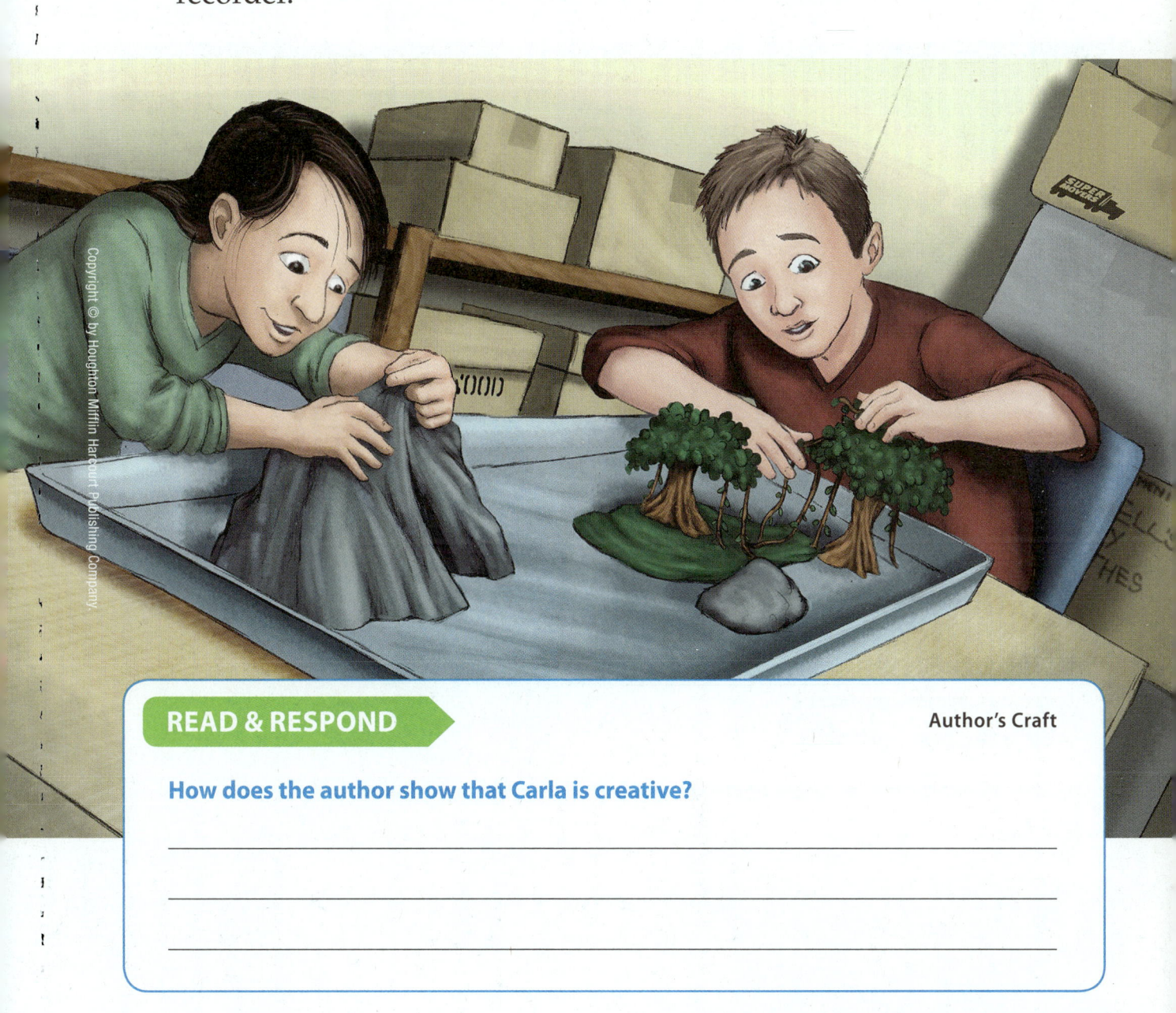

READ & RESPOND

Author's Craft

How does the author show that Carla is creative?

___
___
___

167

In class, Wendell put on the tape and moved the boats around as Carla spoke. The burbling sound and the gliding boats made the model come to life.

Afterward, Carla and Wendell let their amazed classmates see the model up close.

"How did you do it?" Ben asked Carla. "After last year's boat flop, I didn't think you could make a thing!"

"Carla planned it all," Wendell boasted.

"Well, Wendell made the plan work," Carla insisted. "Without him, the boats would have sunk like stones."

READ & RESPOND

Author's Craft

Give an example that shows how the author uses vivid, expressive language.

_____
_____
_____

Reread and Respond

1 **How does Carla feel about working with Wendell at first?**
_____
_____
_____

Hint
For clues, see pages 163 and 164.

2 **What does Wendell contribute to the project?**
_____
_____
_____

Hint
Look for clues on pages 166 and 167.

3 **What does Carla learn about Wendell through her teamwork with him?**
_____
_____
_____

Hint
For a clue, see page 167.

4 **Do you think "Teamwork Week" was a success for Carla and Wendell? Explain your answer.**
_____
_____
_____

Hint
You can find clues throughout the story.

MODULE 8 WEEK 1

Stonehenge: A Riddle

by Mia Lewis

Stonehenge is a circle of tall stones. It is about 80 miles west of London, in England. This circle of stones has fascinated people for thousands of years. There are many other stone circles all over Europe. This one, however, is the most famous.

People study Stonehenge. They write about it. They talk about it. Experts have ideas about who built it. Even so, no one really is sure of who built it, or why.

READ & RESPOND

Main Ideas and Details

Where is Stonehenge located?

_____
_____
_____

Discovering Dates

Archaeologists try to figure out how old ruins are. They dig carefully. They look at the tools the builders used. If the tools are made of stone or bone, the builders probably worked before metal was used.

As people dig, they look for materials that were once part of living things. They look for wood or bone. These can be tested to see how old they are. The digging and the tests have helped scientists figure out when Stonehenge was built. It was a long time ago!

READ & RESPOND

Main Ideas and Details

What is the main idea discussed on this page?

_____
_____
_____

Three Stages

The stones at Stonehenge no longer stand as they once did. Many are missing. Some have fallen. The ones that are left reveal a lot. They show that Stonehenge was carefully planned and built at a very slow pace. It was built over a long period of time.

The stones were set up in three main stages. The stages were many years apart. They are often called Stonehenge I, Stonehenge II, and Stonehenge III. Each stage was different.

READ & RESPOND

Text Structure

Reread the second paragraph on this page. If you were the author of this text, how would you organize information about the three main stages of Stonehenge?

_____

_____

Stonehenge I

Many people underestimated the age of Stonehenge. Archaeologists now think that workers began building about 3100 B.C.E. That's more than 5,000 years ago! They began by digging a round ditch. The ditch, extending about twenty feet from side to side, was about six feet deep.

Workers dug fifty-six holes inside the ditch. They filled in the holes with dirt. Nobody is sure what the purpose of the holes was.

| READ & RESPOND | Main Ideas and Details |

Give three details about the first stage of building at Stonehenge.

_____
_____
_____

Stonehenge II

The second building stage took place around 2100 B.C.E. Workers put about eighty rocks in the center of the site. These rocks are called bluestones, because of their color.

The bluestones are the smallest rocks at Stonehenge. Still, each one weighs several tons. They probably came from mountains in Wales, about 240 miles away. There were no carts with wheels back then. Maybe the stones were carried over water. Maybe workers used log rollers to drag the stones over land. No one is sure.

READ & RESPOND

Text Structure

What do you see that gives you clues about the text structure?

_____
_____
_____

Stonehenge III

More giant stone blocks were added to Stonehenge between 2000 B.C.E. and 1500 B.C.E. Workers built a circle of upright stones. They put a ring of flat stones on top. One flat stone topped each pair of upright stones. Nobody knows exactly how the builders lifted the heavy stones.

In the more recent past, people took stones from Stonehenge to build houses. Now half of the stones are fallen or missing. Even so, Stonehenge is an awesome sight.

READ & RESPOND

Text Structure

How does the text structure the author chose help readers understand how Stonehenge was built?

_____
_____

More Questions

Scientists have reasoned that Stonehenge was very important in its time. Many workers were needed to carry the stones. Many more were needed to shape the stones and put them up. New rocks were added over a fifteen-hundred-year period.

Maybe the building was for important religious events. Again, no one knows for sure. Undoubtedly, people will keep coming up with ideas about Stonehenge. My bet is that the circle of stones will remain a riddle.

READ & RESPOND

Text Structure

Do you think the author chose an effective text structure to share the information in this text? Explain.

_____
_____

Reread and Respond

1 **How long ago did people first start building at Stonehenge?**

_____

_____

_____

> **Hint**
> For a clue, see page 173.

2 **How far did the people move the bluestones to Stonehenge?**

_____

_____

_____

> **Hint**
> For a clue, see page 174.

3 **How do scientists know that Stonehenge was not just an ordinary building?**

_____

_____

_____

> **Hint**
> For clues, see page 176.

4 **What is the main idea of this selection?**

_____

_____

_____

> **Hint**
> Look through the whole passage.

MODULE 8 WEEK 2

In the Year 2525

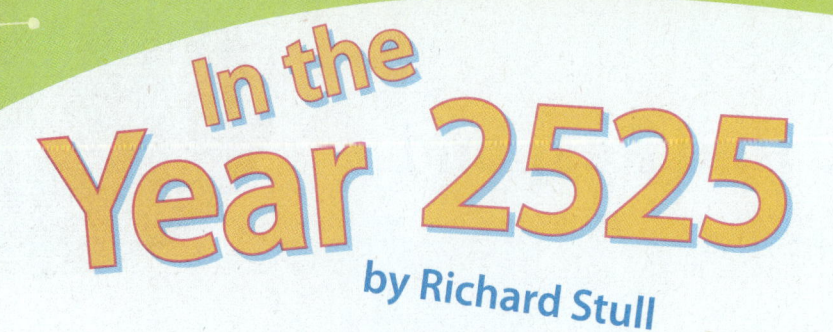

by Richard Stull

Vacations in the year 2525 are not what they used to be. In the past, people packed a car and drove for hours or days. Now people can travel millions of miles without taking a step. They can also travel far back in time.

The Ortiz family wanted to take such a vacation. The first step was a visit to the office of Virtual Vacations. There, they talked with a travel agent named Jill.

READ & RESPOND

Literary Elements

When does this story take place? What details are used to describe it?

_____
_____
_____

"We want to have lots of fun," said Mr. Ortiz.

"We also want to see strange sights," said Mrs. Ortiz.

"I have the perfect destination for you," said Jill. "You're going to Volcano Vacationland!"

Jill explained that Volcano Vacationland was in the distant past. She said that it had pools heated by hot lava and lots of rides for the kids. "You'll also see active volcanoes and dinosaurs," she said. "Of course, the trip is completely safe."

> **READ & RESPOND**
>
> Make Inferences
>
> **Why does Jill assure the Ortiz family that the trip is safe? Explain.**
>
> _____
> _____

179

Jill led the Ortizes into the Virtual Vacation Room. In this room, the setting and feel of a distant place is produced by computers. The computers can also create settings from long ago.

People on a Virtual Vacation feel as if they are really visiting a place. They can do all the things that they would do if they were really there. In fact, they never leave the Virtual Vacation Room.

"Just yell when you want to come home," said Jill. "I'll be at the controls."

READ & RESPOND

Make Inferences

Why do you think the author wrote this story?

_____
_____
_____

180

Suddenly, the Ortizes were staring at a strange being with two heads. It was sleeping on a couch. "This isn't very exciting," said Mrs. Ortiz. "I don't see any volcanoes."

Like their parents, the Ortiz children were not impressed by the snoring being with two heads. "Where are all the fun rides?" they asked.

The Ortizes could see that they were not at Volcano Vacationland. They yelled for Jill to bring them back.

READ & RESPOND

Literary Elements

What happens first to the Ortizes in the Virtual Vacation Room?

_____
_____
_____

181

"I must have pushed the wrong button," admitted Jill. "I think I sent you to the planet Frufee by mistake." The Ortizes decided to try again.

Soon they heard what sounded like gunfire. Suddenly, a soldier was shouting at them. "This can't be right," said Mr. Ortiz. "It looks more like the American Revolution."

They yelled again for Jill to bring them back.

"I'm sorry," she said. "I must have pushed the buttons for a battle in 1781."

READ & RESPOND

Literary Elements

How would you describe Jill?

_____
_____
_____

"I promise to get it right this time," said Jill. She carefully pushed the buttons.

The Ortizes huddled together in suspense. Each of them wondered what would happen this time. Would they meet another weird being? Would they find themselves in the middle of a battle?

Then a strange landscape came into view.

| READ & RESPOND | Make Inferences |

Why do you think the Ortizes huddled together?

_____
_____
_____

The Ortizes saw volcanoes. They saw fun rides. They saw swimming pools surrounded by hot lava. They even seemed to be riding in a car.

"Hurray!" yelled the Ortizes. "We're finally at Volcano Vacationland."

"It seems that Jill has pushed the right buttons," said Mrs. Ortiz.

Of course, the Ortizes were just standing in the Virtual Vacation Room. They had forgotten that. They were on their fun vacation at last.

READ & RESPOND

Literary Elements

Where does the end of the story take place?

_____
_____
_____

Reread and Respond

1. What settings are there in the story?
   _____
   _____
   _____

   Hint
   You can find clues on almost every page.

2. What happens to the Ortizes the first two times they try to go on their vacation?
   _____
   _____
   _____

   Hint
   For clues, see pages 181 and 182.

3. How are the Ortizes finally able to visit Volcano Vacationland?
   _____
   _____
   _____

   Hint
   For clues, see pages 183 and 184.

4. If you could go on a Virtual Vacation, where would you go? Why?
   _____
   _____
   _____

   Hint
   Part of your answer to question 1 and details in the story should help you.

MODULE 8 WEEK 3

Orphan Boy and the Elk Dogs

by Duncan Searl

No one knew where Orphan Boy had come from. His clothes were rags, and he ate scraps that no one wanted. The children in the village would not play with him. The grown-ups did not trust him or want him in their tepees. So Orphan Boy lived in the bushes at the margins of the village.

At night, Orphan Boy edged closer to the campfires. One old woman was sometimes kind to him. She gave the hungry boy food and sometimes let him sit near her fire.

READ & RESPOND

Theme

Do you think any characters will change or learn anything by the end of the story? Explain.

_____
_____

One night, the woman told Orphan Boy about the Elk Dogs. "Far away to the south," she explained, "the people live under a giant lake. These people keep animals that are as big as Elk and as loyal and as hardworking as Dog!"

Orphan Boy was astonished. How could people live under a lake? Could there really be an animal as big as Elk and as hardworking as Dog?

"If we had Elk Dogs," the woman said, "our people would be strong and free." Then she added sadly, "Our greatest hunters have traveled to this lake to get the Elk Dogs, but they have never returned."

READ & RESPOND Ask and Answer Questions

What questions did Orphan Boy have about the woman's story? Write one more question he might have.

That night, Orphan Boy made a decision. He would get Elk Dogs for the village. At dawn, he set out.

For thirty days, Orphan Boy walked steadily south. He crossed high mountains and cold, deep rivers. He walked until his feet bled. Hungry, lonely, and exhausted, he finally came to a lake.

"You're late!" said a voice. Orphan Boy spun around. A kingfisher was talking to him! "Come with me," the big bird urged. "Grandfather is waiting!" Then it dove into the lake and disappeared.

READ & RESPOND   Theme

What do you learn about Orphan Boy on this page?

_____
_____
_____

Orphan Boy stared at the cold lake water. Should he follow the talking bird? "If I do," the boy reasoned, "I might disappear like the other hunters who came for the Elk Dogs."

Putting aside his fears, Orphan Boy dove into the dark water. He did not even get wet! Somehow the water moved away, and he found himself in front of a giant tepee.

The kingfisher sat on top of the tepee. "Enter Grandfather's tepee," the bird said.

Inside, the tepee was warm and dark. At one end sat the old grandfather. He wore a long, dark robe, and his white hair fell to his shoulders.

READ & RESPOND

Ask and Answer Questions

Write one question you have after reading this page.

_____
_____
_____

Pots of food suddenly appeared on the floor, and Orphan Boy ate hungrily. "You are different from the others who tried to come here," the grandfather told him. "At the lake, they became afraid and deserted. You, however, were brave enough to dive into the water. Because you are brave, your life will be spared."

Just then, Orphan Boy saw two Elk Dogs through the open tepee door. One was as black as night; the other was brown with snow-white spots. Tall and sleek, they raced through the golden grass.

Orphan Boy also saw the kingfisher outside. Somehow the bird had changed into a boy. "Come and ride with me!" the boy called.

READ & RESPOND

Theme

Why is Orphan Boy's life spared?

The two boys climbed onto Elk Dogs and galloped down the valley. They rode for hours. Later, as they rested, Orphan Boy said, "I want to bring some Elk Dogs home with me."

"Grandfather will not just give them to you," the kingfisher boy warned. "However, if you find out his secret, he will give you any gift you want. Try to see his feet under his long robe. Then you will know his secret."

For six days, Orphan Boy stayed in the grandfather's tepee. He never saw the old man's feet. The long black robe always covered them. Finally, it was time for Orphan Boy to leave the mysterious land under the lake.

READ & RESPOND

Ask and Answer Questions

Do you understand what Orphan Boy must do to receive his gift? Write it in your own words.

As Orphan Boy said goodbye, he knelt down at the old man's feet to thank him. As he did, he gently moved aside the edge of the robe. Orphan Boy's eyes widened. Instead of human feet, the grandfather had the shiny hooves of an Elk Dog!

"Ahhh! You know my secret!" the grandfather exclaimed. "Now you can ask for a gift."

■ ■ ■

The ride home was easy, and Orphan Boy did not arrive empty-handed! When the villagers saw his Elk Dogs, they invited Orphan Boy into their tepees. They gave him gifts and food and called him by his real name at last. Everyone agreed that Long Arrow was the greatest hunter of all!

READ & RESPOND

Theme

How did Orphan Boy earn the Elk Dogs for his village?

Reread and Respond

1 **Why do the people in the village call the animals in the south Elk Dogs? What is our name for this animal?**

_____
_____
_____

> **Hint**
> See pages 187 and 191.

2 **How do the peoples' opinions of Orphan Boy change during the story? Why does this change occur?**

_____
_____
_____

> **Hint**
> See pages 186 and 192.

3 **What overall message does this story teach?**

_____
_____
_____

> **Hint**
> Almost every page will help you figure out the theme of the story.

4 **What is Orphan Boy's real name?**

_____
_____
_____

> **Hint**
> For a clue, see page 192.

MODULE 9
WEEK 1

The All-Wrong All-Stars

by Selena Rodo

"You can't convince me to do it," I said to my mom, gazing out the window to hide my feelings.

"Selena, you sing so well. I'd be sad to see you waste your talent," she said.

"So you like my crowing?" I said, frowning.

"You sing!" Mom was quick to respond. "You do *not* crow. Honey, just think about it before you say no."

"I'll sleep on it," I said. The truth is, I felt kind of intimidated to join such a well-known group.

READ & RESPOND

Figurative Language

What example of figurative language does Selena use to describe her singing? Explain.

_____
_____

The All-City Glee Club was the best showcase around for singers. They were all male, but now females could be a part of the group. Yesterday, Mr. Willow asked Inez, Yolanda, and me to join. He said he wanted female voices as an element of the show.

At first, I said no. I didn't think their style would suit me. The All-City Glee Club tends to sing low notes with a slow beat. My talent was singing high notes with a fast beat. I didn't think my singing would fit in with theirs at all. Also, there were bound to be some fans who wouldn't be happy to see girls in the group.

READ & RESPOND

Figurative Language

Give one example of figurative language found on this page.

_____
_____
_____

The next morning, I looked out my window. The last snow of the winter had melted. Small green buds had started to grow on the trees. Maybe it was time for me to grow, too!

"Mom, I'm going to sing with All-City," I said. "I think that I need to at least give it a try."

My mom was all smiles. "Good for you, Selena. I know you can do this."

Later, in class, Mr. Willow explained that the All-City Glee Club would now be called the All-City All-Stars. We were thrilled to be a part of this new group.

READ & RESPOND

Figurative Language

What does it mean to be "all smiles"?

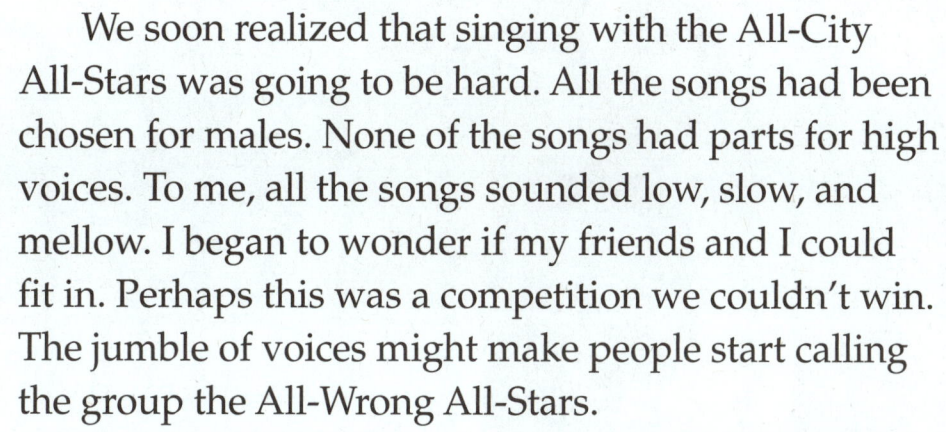

We soon realized that singing with the All-City All-Stars was going to be hard. All the songs had been chosen for males. None of the songs had parts for high voices. To me, all the songs sounded low, slow, and mellow. I began to wonder if my friends and I could fit in. Perhaps this was a competition we couldn't win. The jumble of voices might make people start calling the group the All-Wrong All-Stars.

"I think this is a mistake," I said to Dad after school. "There are no parts in their songs for our high voices. When all of us sing together, it sounds terrible!"

"Don't give up, Selena," Dad declared. "Find a way to show what you can do."

READ & RESPOND

Literary Elements

How does Selena feel about singing with the All-City All-Stars?

_____
_____
_____

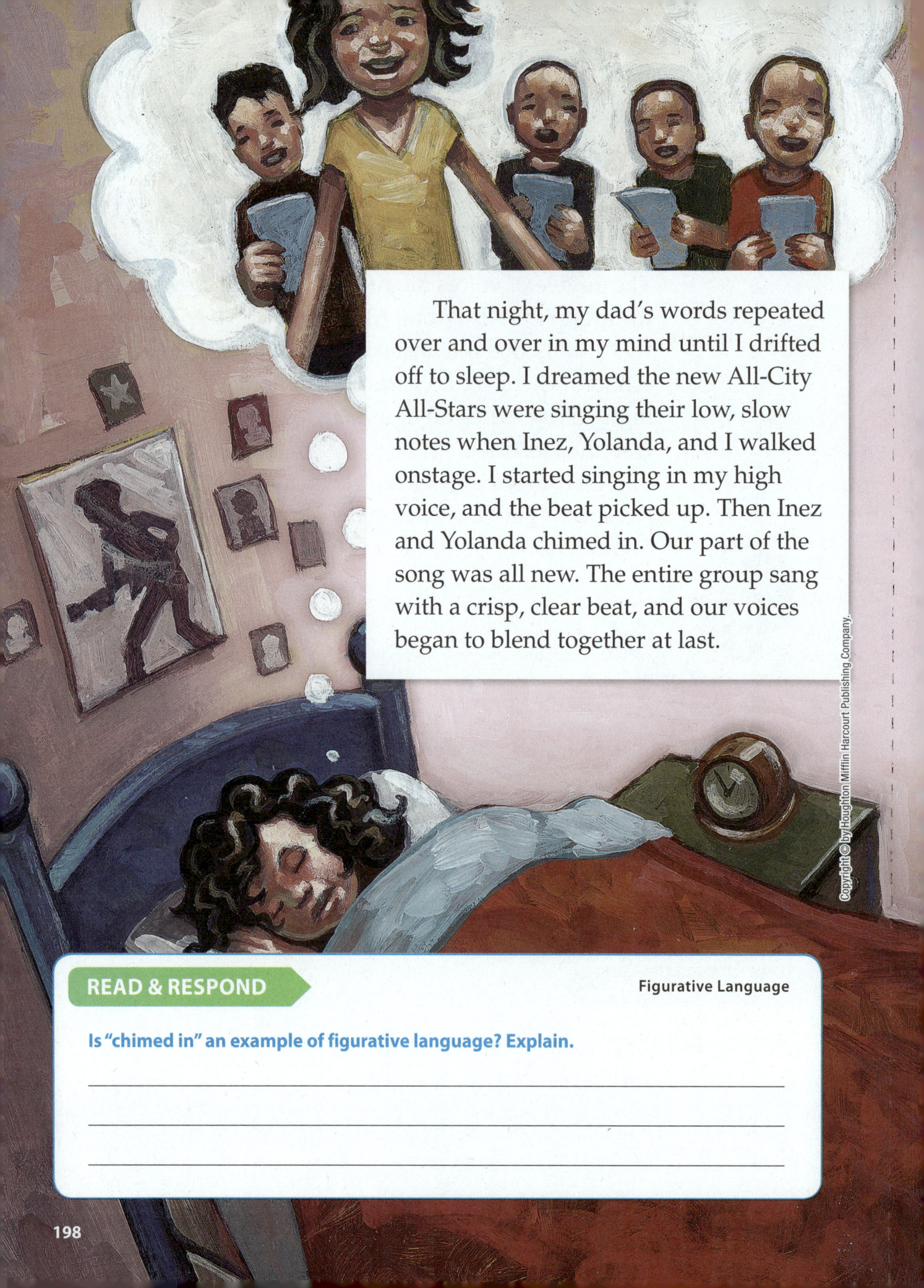

That night, my dad's words repeated over and over in my mind until I drifted off to sleep. I dreamed the new All-City All-Stars were singing their low, slow notes when Inez, Yolanda, and I walked onstage. I started singing in my high voice, and the beat picked up. Then Inez and Yolanda chimed in. Our part of the song was all new. The entire group sang with a crisp, clear beat, and our voices began to blend together at last.

READ & RESPOND

Figurative Language

Is "chimed in" an example of figurative language? Explain.

_____
_____
_____

When I woke up, that new part of the song was still fresh in my mind. I rushed to find Yolanda and Inez and sang the new part to them the same way I had sung it in my dream. Yolanda and Inez followed my lead, and the result was beautiful. Now, we realized, we had to show Mr. Willow and the rest of the All-City All-Stars what we wanted to do. The question was, would they agree?

When we demonstrated our plan, Mr. Willow and the All-City All-Stars stopped and smiled. Mr. Willow said that he had been thinking about how to get our voices to fit in better, too. They all agreed that adding this new part to the song would blend our high voices with their low ones. So, we started a new routine.

READ & RESPOND

Literary Elements

Have you seen any changes in the characters of this story? Explain.

In just two weeks, we had mastered the song and were ready for our first All-City All-Stars show.

As we started to sing, I watched the effect we were having on the audience. Some smiled and leaned toward us, as if they wanted to hear more. Some nodded with the beat. They all seemed to like the way our high and low voices blended. Best of all, when the song ended, they wouldn't stop clapping. We were not all wrong after all! We had truly become the All-City All-Stars.

READ & RESPOND

Literary Elements

What is this story's resolution?

_____
_____
_____

Reread and Respond

1 How does the author's mother feel about her joining the All-City Glee Club?
_____
_____
_____

Hint
For clues, look on page 194.

2 At first, what makes it so difficult for the girls to sing with the group?
_____
_____
_____

Hint
For a clue, see page 197.

3 Is the advice the author's father gives her good or bad? Explain.
_____
_____
_____

Hint
See page 197 and the following pages.

4 Does the audience like the All-City All-Stars? How can you tell?
_____
_____
_____

Hint
For clues, see page 200.

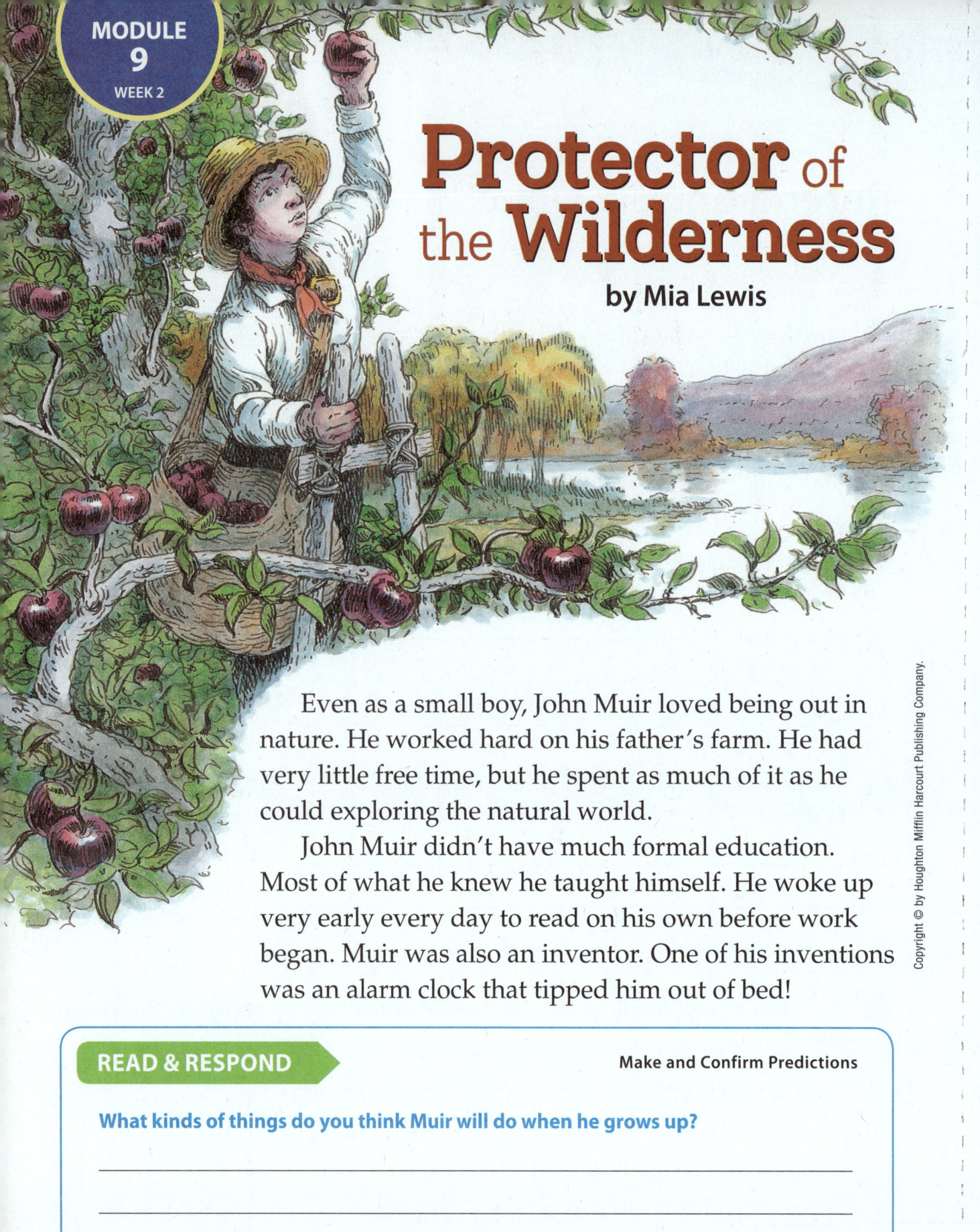

Protector of the Wilderness
by Mia Lewis

Even as a small boy, John Muir loved being out in nature. He worked hard on his father's farm. He had very little free time, but he spent as much of it as he could exploring the natural world.

John Muir didn't have much formal education. Most of what he knew he taught himself. He woke up very early every day to read on his own before work began. Muir was also an inventor. One of his inventions was an alarm clock that tipped him out of bed!

READ & RESPOND

Make and Confirm Predictions

What kinds of things do you think Muir will do when he grows up?

_____
_____
_____

Later, Muir went to a university for a few years. Soon he left it, saying he preferred the "University of the Wilderness." He hiked to Canada, where he worked in a broom factory. He returned to the United States after the factory burned down.

Muir was working in Indiana when he injured his eye. For one scary month, he could not see, but his injury changed his life. He decided to travel and spend as much time outside as possible. He set out on a 1,000-mile trek to the Gulf of Mexico.

READ & RESPOND

Ideas and Support

Why does the author put the phrase "University of the Wilderness" inside quotation marks?

_____

_____

Muir spent much of the next forty years hiking around. In one expedition after another, he explored wild places. He found some mountains that he loved out West. In this mountain range was Muir's favorite place of all, Yosemite Valley.

Muir spent a lot of time at Yosemite. He got to know all about the valley's geology and ecology. He soon became a guide there. People came from all across the country for tours.

READ & RESPOND

Make and Confirm Predictions

Are the predictions you made earlier still accurate? Do you need to make adjustments? Explain.

_____
_____

Muir was more than just a tour guide for Yosemite. He also worked to protect the area. He wanted it to stay wild. He was happy when Congress created Yosemite National Park. No one would be allowed to develop the land.

Yosemite wasn't Muir's only concern. He founded the Sierra Club to save all wild places. The club worked to protect natural areas. It is still going strong!

READ & RESPOND

Make and Confirm Predictions

What other things do you think Muir did to protect the land? Why do you think so?

_____
_____
_____

After he married, Muir moved to a farm and had two children. He was not happy staying in one place. He soon resumed his travels and his writing.

In all, Muir wrote ten books and three hundred magazine articles. The articles came out in all the major magazines of the day. This meant that his words reached a large group of people. They paid attention to what he had to say.

READ & RESPOND

Ideas and Support

What do you think is the author's opinion of Muir? Why do you think so?

_____
_____
_____

Some people value land for the ways they can make money from it. Muir said that untouched land was valuable. He thought that unspoiled wilderness is the greatest treasure of all.

Muir's ideas changed the way people thought. They even changed how the President of the United States thought. President Theodore Roosevelt spent three days camping with Muir. He listened to Muir's ideas, and later he set aside land for national parks, forests, and monuments.

READ & RESPOND

Ideas and Support

Is this statement a fact or an opinion: "Unspoiled wilderness is the greatest treasure of all." Explain.

_____
_____

John Muir changed our country. He worked to save Yosemite and many other wild areas. The goals he fought for were fulfilled when Congress created the National Park Service. That was just two years after Muir died. Today, everyone can visit the National Parks.

Muir fought his whole life to protect the environment. What if John Muir were alive today? He would be a very busy man!

| READ & RESPOND | Ideas and Support |

What does the author mean when she says John Muir would be a busy man if he were alive today?

_____
_____

Reread and Respond

1 How did an accident change John Muir's life forever?
_____
_____
_____

Hint
For a clue, see pages 203.

2 What was the author's purpose for writing about John Muir?
_____
_____
_____

Hint
Clues are on every page!

3 What details support the idea that Muir had a major impact on the country and its people?
_____
_____
_____

Hint
Clues are on every page!

4 What are some things that Muir started or worked for in his lifetime that are still around today?
_____
_____
_____

Hint
For clues, see pages 205, 207, and 208.

MODULE 9 WEEK 3

Off to Oregon

by Sheila Boyle

"Maybe you're wondering what's been going on in the store?" Papa asked as we began eating dinner.

"Do you mean all the cleaning and packing?" I asked.

"I've sold the store," Papa said. "Everything here feels too cramped. We're joining a group of families and moving west."

"Leave the city?" The question stuck in my throat.

"Anneke, my dear," Papa whispered. "The government is offering free land out West. If we don't move now, we may never have another chance."

READ & RESPOND

Author's Craft

How does the author use dialogue to tell you more about the characters? Give evidence from the text to support at least one example.

_____

_____

A week later my room was empty, and all my favorite things had been sold to strangers. Only essentials could go in the wagon. Everything else had to be left behind.

As we passed the store on our way out of the city, Papa showed no regrets. He remained cheerful even when we had to get rid of more of our possessions. Mama's cooking stove was left by the side of the road. Beside it were my inks and paints. I had one quill left, tucked into the lining of my dress.

> **READ & RESPOND**
>
> Point of View
>
> **Is the writer using first-person point of view or third-person point of view? How do you know?**
>
> _____
> _____

Finally, after six long, hard weeks of traveling, we reached Independence, Missouri. People filled the street, clustering around supply stores and trading posts.

I watched as an Indian girl about my age came out of a shop. Her eyes met mine, and she smiled. I sat down beside her. "Hi," I said, smiling. "Anneke," I said, tapping my chest.

"Geyohi," she said. "Me." She slipped a string of tiny blue beads off her wrist and slid it onto mine. I untied a yellow ribbon from my pigtail and tied it in her hair. I had to leave to help restock our wagon, and when I returned, she had vanished.

READ & RESPOND

Author's Craft

What mood does the author create in this section of text? Explain.

_____
_____
_____

I thought I had made a new friend, but then suddenly she was gone. Now, all I had to look forward to was the rest of our journey. We had 2,000 miles to go. It would take five months.

Almost from the start, we fared badly. My little sister, Petra, had a terrible mishap as the wagon train tried to cross a river. Water surged through the rapids. The ferrymen put the wagons, one by one, on a raft. The oxen swam across. When it was our turn, I heard a scream. Petra had fallen into the water!

"Petra! Head for Rorie!" I yelled, pointing to my favorite ox. Swimming against the current, Petra reached the ox and held tight until he reached the other side.

READ & RESPOND

Point of View

How would this part of the story be different if it were written from Petra's point of view?

_____
_____

213

The next few weeks passed in a blur. We endured the torment of pelting rain. No matter how we tried to keep the wagons waterproof, the rain found its way in.

Then the land changed. There were no trees, only massive rocks and the dry, scorching prairie. Sometimes at night people talked about what they would build on their new land. I asked, "Does no one live there now?"

"Indians lived there," said the wagon train boss, "but they're gone now." The government had promised the land to the Indians forever. Now the government was breaking its promise.

I walked away, angry. What about Geyohi? Her family needed land, too.

READ & RESPOND

Point of View

Would you know that Anneke was angry if the story was told from a different perspective? Explain.

_____

_____

One day, we crossed the top of a hill. Fort Hall shone in the early morning sunlight like a beacon. We had reached Oregon!

Soon the landscape was lush, green, and full of trees. People cheered. Men threw their hats. Some of them kissed the ground.

My family spent two hard months clearing trees off pasture land. Winter came, and we were still living in our small tarpaper hut. The best news is Papa. He is happy and has great plans for the future. Here he'll build the barn. There, the farmhouse. Over there, the stables.

For my birthday, he had a special surprise for me: a bottle of ink, so I can write in my journal.

READ & RESPOND

Author's Craft

How does the author show the relationship between Anneke and her father? Give examples from the text.

How Far in a Day?

On many days, the wagon train would only cover ten to fifteen miles. On rainy or muddy days, it might travel only a single mile. It would take these pioneers five to seven days to travel the distance we can drive by car in a single hour.

Life and Death on the Oregon Trail

Nearly one in ten people who set off on the Oregon Trail did not survive. The two biggest causes of death were disease and accidents.

Hard Weather

Fierce thunderstorms, huge hailstones, high winds, snowstorms, lightning, tornadoes, and desert heat persuaded many travelers to turn back.

READ & RESPOND Main Ideas and Details

How do these facts help you better understand the courage and resourcefulness of the early pioneers?

_____

_____

Reread and Respond

1 What caused people to undertake such a hard journey across the country in covered wagons?

_____
_____
_____

> **Hint**
> For clues, see page 210.

2 How did Anneke help save Petra's life?

_____
_____
_____

> **Hint**
> For a clue, see page 213.

3 How would you describe Anneke's father?

_____
_____
_____

> **Hint**
> For clues, see pages 210 and 215.

4 What effect do you think traveling west will have on Anneke? Explain your answer.

_____
_____
_____

> **Hint**
> Clues you can use are on almost every page.

Nothing Ever Happens in the Country

by Shawn Boyle

A few months ago, Mom and Dad told me that we would be moving to the country. They were tired of the frantic pace of city life. They wanted some peace and quiet. So, they had decided that we would live out in the middle of nowhere. On a farm!

As for me, I didn't want to go. I knew that I'd be bored all the time. Everyone knows nothing ever happens in the country.

I was right. It didn't take me very long to realize that I didn't like the country one bit.

READ & RESPOND

Literary Elements

Do you think the setting will be important to the story? Explain.

_____
_____
_____

Even my birthday on the farm was boring. In the city, I would have had all my friends over, and we would have had a great time. In the country, the only kid who came to my party was the goat! He tried to steal my birthday cake right off the picnic table.

Mom told me that I'd make lots of new friends when school started. I just shrugged my shoulders. Then Mom and Dad told me that they had a surprise for me. They had arranged for my best friend Kwan to come visit for a week. That was really great news.

READ & RESPOND

Theme

How does the narrator feel about the country? Do you think he will change his mind? Explain.

_____

_____

219

It was only a few days until Kwan would arrive, but it seemed like years. Mom kept telling me to go outside and enjoy the sunshine. Why would I? I didn't feel like sharing my meals with the goat. I didn't need to have a romp with the barnyard chickens.

As I listened to Mom, I kept reading my comic books and picturing life in the city. I missed the noise—the honking horns, the sirens, the loud buses.

READ & RESPOND

Literary Elements

What can you tell about the narrator from his thoughts about going outside?

_____
_____
_____

Finally, Kwan arrived. Dad and I met him at the train station. I warned him that he could expect a really boring week, but he was really excited. He had never been to a farm before. On the ride home, he could not hide his enthusiasm. He pointed at a wild turkey on the side of the road, at a groundhog chewing grass, and even at a herd of cows.

Still, I was sure that Kwan would soon find out how boring life on a farm really was.

READ & RESPOND

Literary Elements

What do Kwan's reactions to the country tell you about him?

_____
_____
_____

The next morning, Kwan was up at the crack of dawn. I watched him bounding over to the chicken coop, and then I followed him at a slower pace.

Kwan was thrilled to find a couple of eggs there. "Talk about fresh!" he said. "Boy, this is the life."

I wasn't sure that having eggs for breakfast was such an amazing event, but Kwan's good mood rubbed off on me. It didn't last very long, though. Kwan wanted to go for a hike. What could be duller than that? As he was my best friend, I pretended to be excited.

READ & RESPOND

Theme

What shows that Kwan's behavior is beginning to change the narrator's attitude?

_____
_____
_____

Mom had packed us lunch and had made sure we took binoculars with us. I couldn't imagine why we would need them. I didn't think it would take very long for Kwan to get bored, binoculars or no binoculars.

I was wrong. Everything Kwan saw amazed him. Birds, trees, grass, everything made him happy. Then he tugged at my sleeve and pointed up at the sky at some hawks circling. We both grabbed our binoculars. The birds were awesome! Suddenly, we saw one of the hawks lunging toward the ground. The next second, it flew back up with a tiny mouse in its claws. The hike wasn't so bad, after all.

READ & RESPOND

Literary Elements

What changes the narrator's feelings about the hike?

_____
_____
_____

Our trip through the woods got even better. We saw a tree so filled with termites it was ready to fall down. We heard a hammering noise and looked up to see a woodpecker. In the next tree there was a beehive. A little later we saw a fox and some skunks. We didn't get too close to the skunks!

We were both exhausted when we got home. Before we went to bed, we talked about what we would do the next day, and the next. Slowly it dawned on me—living in the country was as exciting as I would let it be. It had taken a city boy to show me!

| READ & RESPOND | Theme |

How has the narrator changed by the end of the story? What happened to change him?

_____
_____

Reread and Respond

1 **What is the theme of the story?**

_____

_____

_____

> **Hint**
> Think about how the narrator changed.

2 **Could this story have taken place in a different setting? Explain.**

_____

_____

_____

> **Hint**
> Reread the story to help you.

3 **What can you tell about Kwan's character?**

_____

_____

_____

> **Hint**
> For clues, see pages 221 through 224.

4 **How do the narrator and Kwan differ?**

_____

_____

_____

> **Hint**
> Clues are on every page.

Will the American Chestnut Survive?

by Dina McClellan

*Under a spreading chestnut tree
The village smithy stands;
The smith, a mighty man is he,
With large and sinewy hands . . .*

—from "The Village Blacksmith" by Henry Wadsworth Longfellow (1807–1882)

A Celebrated Tree

The American chestnut tree was one of the most celebrated forest trees in the northeastern United States. It once grew across millions of acres from Maine to Mississippi. At 110 feet tall, these trees dwarfed all others. The Appalachians were so thickly covered with them that when they flowered, the mountaintops turned white. In the fall, the earth was black with fallen chestnuts.

READ & RESPOND

Central Idea

Reread the title of this text. Explain what you think the central idea of this text will be.

_____
_____
_____

A Mysterious Fungus

Today, the presence of the American chestnut in the region has been reduced to almost nothing. The reason is a mysterious fungus. It was first discovered in 1904 at the Bronx Zoo in New York City. Within two years, all the chestnut trees at the zoo were dead or dying. In another fifty years, the fungus would kill four billion trees across the eastern United States.

This is a fungus that spreads easily. Puffs of spores (tiny, seed-like particles that can grow into a fungus) fly through the air and are transferred to the fur and feathers of animals. When these animals perch on chestnut trees, the spores can settle in the cracks in the bark. The fungus grows around the tree and strangles it.

READ & RESPOND

Text Structure

What is causing the American chestnut tree to die?

_____
_____
_____

But all is not lost. The American chestnut has two things going for it: (1) the fungus can't kill the roots, and (2) the roots can grow into new trees. That's the good news. The bad news is that the fungus still lives in the region and can attack new chestnut growth.

READ & RESPOND

Central Idea

Why might the American chestnut become extinct one day?

_____
_____
_____

HUMANS TO THE RESCUE

In the 1930s, scientists thought the American chestnut could be saved. They discovered the Chinese chestnut, a relative of the American tree. The big difference was that the Chinese chestnut came from the same region as the fungus, so it had a kind of built-in protection. The Chinese chestnut could not get sick.

The scientists cross-bred the two species, hoping the result would be young trees that looked American but didn't get sick. It didn't work, however, and this work ended in the 1970s.

READ & RESPOND

Central Idea

Why did scientists of the 1930s believe that the Chinese chestnut could help solve the problem?

_____

_____

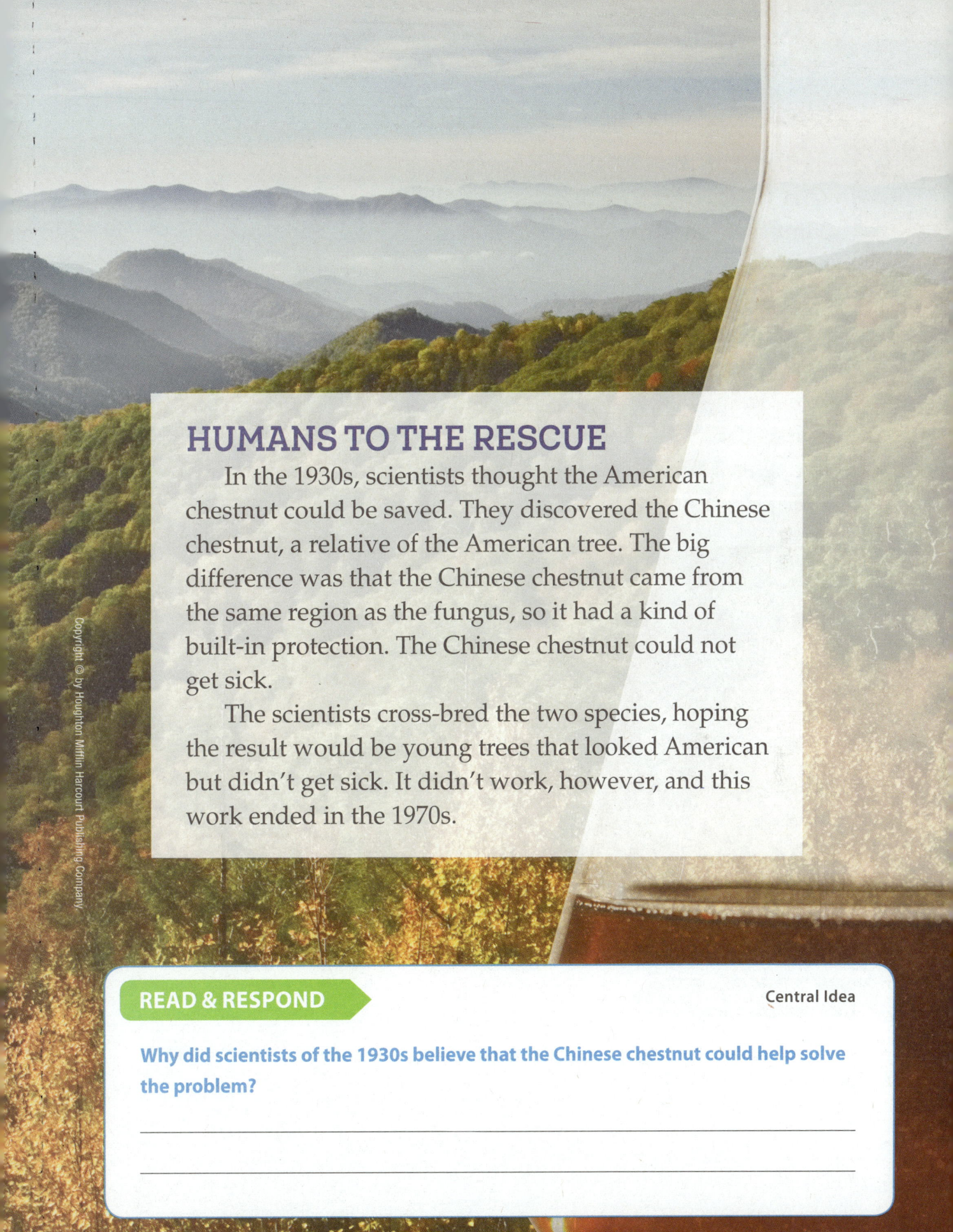

Then, in the 1980s, a scientist named Dr. Charles Burnham teamed up with a Minnesota chestnut farmer to find a new way of breeding the two trees.

First, the Chinese chestnut was crossed with the American chestnut, resulting in young trees that were half Chinese and half American. Then, these young trees were crossed back with the American parent, over and over again. The result of this procedure is an American tree that doesn't get sick.

> **READ & RESPOND**
>
> Text Structure
>
> **What transition words and phrases do you see that give you clues about the text structure?**
>
> _____
> _____

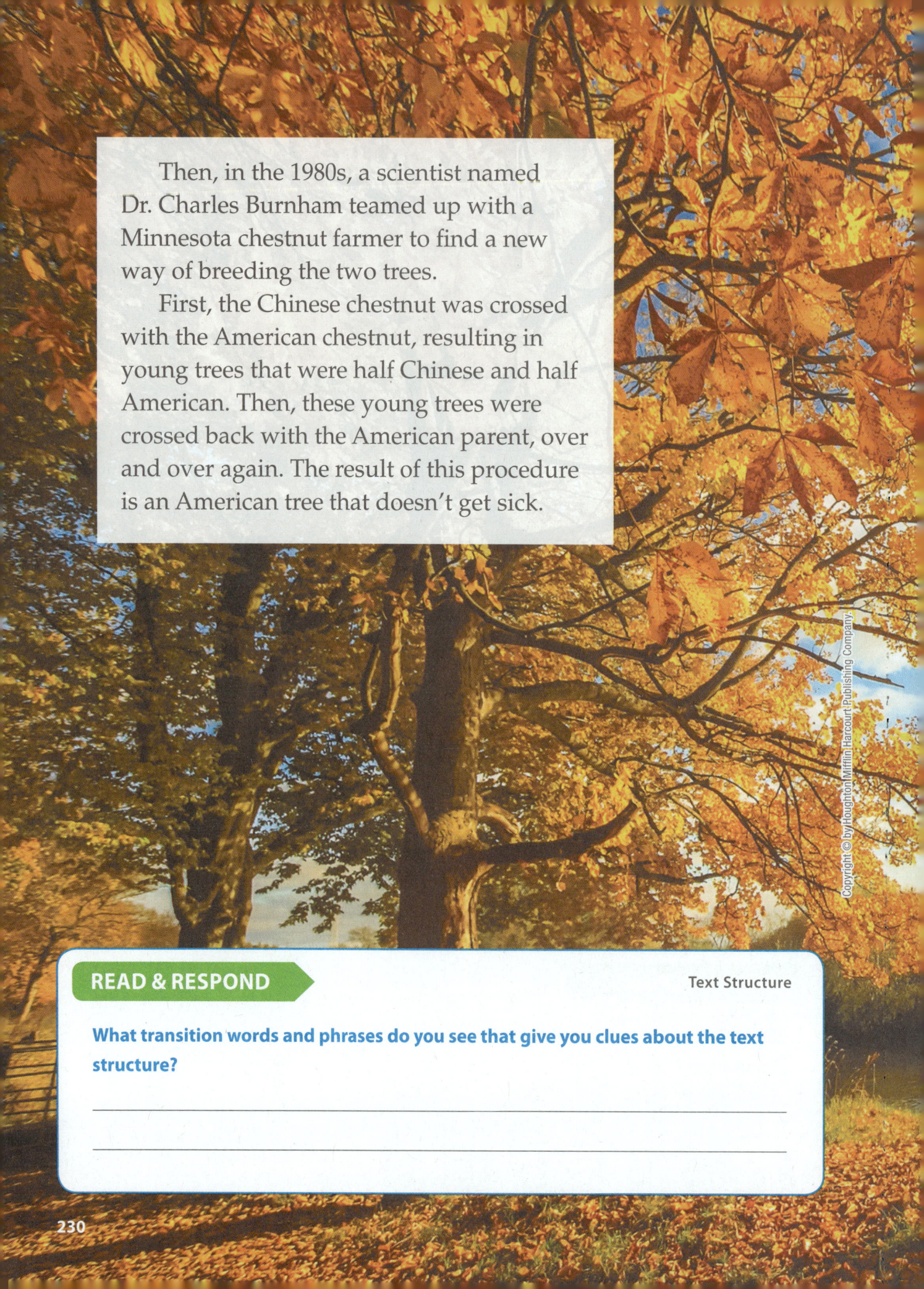

The American Chestnut Foundation

In 1983, an organization called the American Chestnut Foundation was set up to support the program started by Dr. Burnham. Its members are hopeful that once the trees have been bred they can be put back into the forest using a process called reforestation. Then it's up to nature to keep things going.

READ & RESPOND

Text Structure

Do you think the author chose an effective text structure to share the information in this text? Explain.

_____

_____

Hundreds of trees have been reforested in Virginia and Tennessee, and they appear to be doing well. But more time is needed to know if the trees can survive in the long run. Reforestation is a huge task that takes many years of hard work.

Foundation members truly care about these proud and beautiful trees. They believe that someday the famous "spreading chestnut tree" will regain its rightful place in the American forest.

READ & RESPOND

Central Idea

What is the central idea of this text? How do you know?

_____
_____
_____

Reread and Respond

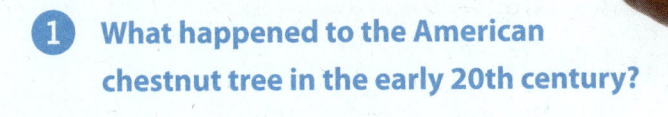

1 What happened to the American chestnut tree in the early 20th century?

_____

_____

_____

Hint

For clues, see pages 226 and 227.

2 How does the fungus kill the trees?

_____

_____

_____

Hint

For a description, see page 227.

3 What makes the Chinese chestnut such a good choice for cross-breeding?

_____

_____

_____

Hint

For clues, see page 229.

4 What are the goals of the American Chestnut Foundation?

_____

_____

_____

Hint

For clues, see page 231.

The Many Faces of Rolling Hills

by Richard Stull

Do you know Rolling Hills? It's a small town near High Falls Park, about twenty miles outside the city. I had hardly given the place a thought until last month. That's when Mom and I went there to visit my aunt.

One great thing about our visit was the peach cobbler that my aunt made. Another great thing was what I learned about Rolling Hills. It gave me a whole new viewpoint on the area. It also made me think differently about the places where people live.

READ & RESPOND

Visualize

What details in the first paragraph help you visualize the town being described by the author?

_____
_____

My aunt moved to Rolling Hills three months ago. Her house looks brand-new. In my mind, the whole town looks brand-new. The streets are lined with houses, so I guess a lot of families live there. I saw kids playing together in the yards and cycling along the streets. It's a great place to live.

READ & RESPOND

Visualize

Does the illustration match the picture that the words on this page paint in your mind? Explain.

_____

_____

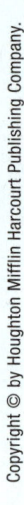

I was in my aunt's yard when I noticed an old building in the distance. Its walls had fallen down. I asked my aunt what the old building was doing in a new neighborhood like Rolling Hills.

My aunt told me that Rolling Hills had not always been like it is now. She said that all of the land around there had previously been a farm. I was amazed. I couldn't believe that all the houses and yards were built on what had once been farmland.

> **READ & RESPOND**
>
> **Main Ideas and Details**
>
> **What was the land around Rolling Hills used for before it was made into a new neighborhood?**
>
> _____
>
> _____

I asked my aunt about other aspects of Rolling Hills that used to be different. Of course, she told me to visit a library to find out. Aunts are always like that. Still, I did as she suggested.

The local librarian helped me find newspaper stories about Rolling Hills. Sure enough, it had once been a big farm with a farmhouse and a barn. Cattle grazed in fields where houses now stand.

READ & RESPOND

Visualize

Explain how the author helps you visualize what Rolling Hills looked like when it was a farm.

_____
_____

Then I got to thinking about what the whole area had been like before it was a farm. This time the librarian pointed out several books about the history of the county. From my reading, I learned that two hundred years ago, Rolling Hills was not a farm at all. It was all forest. There was no park nearby, and there was no city. The library wasn't here, either.

Settlers came here, surveyed the land, and decided that they were the only people around. Of course, they were wrong.

READ & RESPOND

Visualize

Describe the area of Rolling Hills two hundred years ago.

_____
_____
_____

American Indians lived in the area. They had lived here for hundreds of years before the settlers arrived. Back then, all the land in these parts was a thick forest. The people lived here for centuries without changing the land.

The Indians hunted in the forest and fished in the streams. The summers were probably very pretty. The winters were most likely quite harsh.

READ & RESPOND

Visualize

What words on this page help you visualize what the land might have looked like hundreds of years ago?

_____
_____

I know it's hard to believe that this busy town was once completely rural. It's true, though.

So far, I've discovered that Rolling Hills is way more interesting than I would have believed, and I've researched only what the area was like a few hundred years ago. I wonder what it was like a thousand years ago, or ten thousand years ago. There might have been different kinds of trees. The hills might not have been as steep. Maybe musk oxen and mastodons lived here. Perhaps there were even saber-toothed tigers, too!

READ & RESPOND

Main Ideas and Details

What does the writer learn about Rolling Hills?

_____
_____
_____

Reread and Respond

1 What is the writer's opinion of studying local history?

_____

_____

_____

Hint
You can find clues throughout the story.

2 What first got the writer thinking about how places change?

_____

_____

_____

Hint
For clues, see page 236.

3 How is the area of Rolling Hills today different from the way it was two hundred years ago?

_____

_____

_____

Hint
You can find clues throughout the story.

4 Why does the writer's aunt suggest that he visit the local library?

_____

_____

_____

Hint
For clues, see page 237.

Credits

2 *Molly Pitcher firing cannon* ©Niday Picture Library/Alamy; 3 *Independence Hall* ©Corbis; 3 *flag* ©Photodisc/Getty Images; 3 *flag of Great Britain* ©Stockbyte/Getty Images; 3 *doorknob* ©Photodisc/Getty Images; 4 *Lydia Darragh Revolutionary War* ©Science History Images/Alamy; 5 *woman dressed as soldier* ©Science History Images/Alamy; 6 *soldiers shooting* ©VisionsofAmerica/Joe Soehm/Digital Vision/Getty Images; 7 *kettle cooking pot* ©laurien/iStock/Getty Images Plus/Getty Images; 7 *butter churn* ©Comstock/Getty Images; 7 *spinning wheel* ©Comstock/Getty Images; 7 *Join or Die* ©Everett Historical/Shutterstock; 8 *rustic building on river* ©Corbis; 8 *pen & ink* ©Photodisc/Getty Images; 9 *Molly Pitcher firing cannon* ©Niday Picture Library/Alamy; 11 *White House* ©Digital Vision/Getty Images; 11 *chef hat* ©Photodisc/Getty Images; 12 *clipboard* ©2001 Photodisc/Getty Images; 13 *chickens* ©Digital Vision/Getty Images; 14 *watering plant* ©Corbis; 14 *assorted vegetables* ©Houghton Mifflin Harcourt; 15 *child gardening* ©Houghton Mifflin Harcourt; 16 *dictionary* ©Photodisc/Getty Images; 19 *box of popcorn* ©Photodisc/Getty Images; 19 *ticket* ©Photodisc/Getty Images; 20 *notepad and folder* ©Photodisc/Getty Images; 20 *35mm film* ©Artville/Getty Images; 21 *colored pencils* ©Photodisc/Getty Images; 21 *pad* ©Photodisc/Getty Images; 22 *film reel* ©Photodisc/Getty Images; 22 *notepad and folder* ©Photodisc/Getty Images; 23 *pad* ©Photodisc/Getty Images; 23 *camera* ©Photodisc/Getty Images; 24 *35mm film* ©Artville/Getty Images; 24 *composition book* ©Artville/Getty Images; 24 *spotlight* ©Photodisc/Getty Images; 34 *baseball bat* ©Comstock/Getty Images; 35 *baseball glove* ©Photodisc/Getty Images; 35 *baseball team* ©Photodisc/Getty Images; 36 *tickets* ©Houghton Mifflin Harcourt; 36 *baseball stadium* ©Sam Dudgeon/Houghton Mifflin Harcourt; 37 *little league baseball* ©Photodisc/Alamy; 37 *baseball* ©Comstock/Getty Images; 38 *glove* ©Comstock/Getty Images; 38 *school locker* ©Photodisc/Getty Images; 39 *catcher's mask* ©Comstock/Getty Images; 39 *baseball catcher* ©Photodisc/Getty Images; 40 *little league player* ©Photodisc/Getty Images; 40 *baseball glove* ©Comstock/Getty Images; 40 *baseball glove* ©Photodisc/Getty Images; 41 *glove* Comstock/Getty Images; 42 *sparrow* ©Ufulum/Shutterstock; 44 *sparrow* ©Ufulum/Shutterstock; 46-48 *sparrow* ©Ufulum/Shutterstock; 50 *ocean liner* ©nerthuz/Shutterstock; 51 *black duffel* ©Stockbyte/Getty Images; 51 *brown suitcase* ©Stockbyte/Getty Images; 51 *black satchel* ©Stockbyte/Getty Images; 51 *blue duffels* ©Photodisc/Getty Images; 51 *trunk* ©Stockbyte/Getty Images; 51 *backpack* ©Photodisc/Getty Images; 52 *beige suitcase* ©Photodisc/Getty Images; 53 *dolphin* ©Getty Images; 53 *notebook* ©Artville/Getty Images; 53 *pencil pen marker* ©effe 45/Dreamstime; 53 *school supplies* ©margouillat photo/Shutterstock; 54 *white lightning* ©Getty Images; 55 *shell* ©Photodisc/Getty Images; 56 *ocean horizon* ©Don Farrall/Photodisc/Getty Images; 61 *Frederick Douglass* ©Corbis; 73 *crown* ©Photodisc/Getty Images; 90 *bus* ©Victoria Smith/Houghton Mifflin Harcourt; 91 *farm* ©Photodisc/Getty Images; 92 *horse* ©Digital Vision/Getty Images; 93 *horse* ©Digital Vision/Getty Images; 94 *horse* ©Digital Vision/Getty Images; 95 *saddle* ©Comstock/Getty Images; 95 *rope* ©Houghton Mifflin Harcourt; 96 *American quarter horse* ©Philip Nealey/Getty Images; 96 *horseshoe* ©Comstock/Getty Images; 96 *equestrian hat* ©Comstock/Getty Images; 97 *saddle* ©Comstock/Getty Images; 98 *storm over sea* ©Photodisc/Getty Images; 98 *life jacket* ©Photodisc/Getty Images; 99 *cb radio* ©Comstock/Getty Images; 100 *bad weather* ©Digital Vision/Getty Images; 100 *emergency helicopter* ©Szasz-Fabian Jozsef/Shutterstock; 101 *life preserver* ©Comstock/Getty Images; 102 *thunderstorm & rain* ©Getty Images; 102 *rope* ©Comstock/Getty Images; 103 *overturned car* ©Corbis; 104 *flooded neighborhood* ©SlobodanMiljevic/iStock/Getty Images Plus/Getty Images; 104 *doctor's kit* ©Comstock/Getty Images; 105 *emergency helicopter* ©Szasz-Fabian Jozsef/Shutterstock; 106 *alaska landscape* ©Photodisc/Getty Images; 106 *town* ©Photodisc/Getty Images; 107 *snow mountains* ©Photodisc/Getty Images; 107 *fishing boat* ©John A. Rizzo/Photodisc/Getty Images; 108 *dead fish* ©Photodisc/Getty Images; 108 *oil spill* ©Photodisc/Getty Images; 108 *sunset* ©Photodisc/Getty Images; 109 *bears* ©Getty Images; 109 *seagull* ©Stockbyte/Getty Images; 109 *dead fish on shore* ©Africa Studio/Shutterstock; 110 *snow mountains* ©Photodisc/Getty Images; 111 *fishing boat* ©Theunis Jacobus Botha/Shutterstock; 111 *dead bird* ©Photodisc/Getty Images; 111 *oil slick* ©Photodisc/Getty Images; 111 *fishing rod* ©Civdis/Shutterstock; 112 *seagulls* ©Stockbyte/Getty Images; 112 *sunset* ©Photodisc/Getty Images; 113 *dead fish* ©Photodisc/Getty Images; 114-115 *monarch butterfly* ©Siede Preis/Photodisc/Getty Images; 117-118 *monarch butterfly* ©Siede Preis/Photodisc/Getty Images; 122 *lasso* ©Photodisc/Getty Images; 122 *woodgrain* ©Photodisc/Getty Images; 123 *compass* ©Artville/Getty Images; 124 *brown paper* ©Paladin12/Shutterstock; 126 *cowboy boots* ©Photodisc/Getty Images; 127 *frame in gold leaf* ©C Squared Studios/Photodisc/Getty Images; 128 *Death Valley* ©Photodisc/Getty Images; 129 *hat* ©Comstock/Getty Images; 130 *plane* ©Brand X Pictures/Getty Images; 130 *woodgrain* ©Corbis; 131 *drum* ©Photodisc/Getty Images; 134 *drumsticks* ©Artville/Getty Images; 138 *fork and knife* ©Planner/Shutterstock; 139 *baseball* ©Photodisc/Getty Images; 140 *blue school backpack* ©Mike Flippo/Shutterstock; 140 *baseball jersey* ©C Squared Studios/Photodisc/Getty Images; 142 *baseball bat* ©Artville/Getty Images; 142 *baseball helmet* ©Photodisc/Getty Images; 143 *baseball* ©Comstock/Getty Images; 144 *baseball glove* ©C Squared Studios/Photodisc/Getty Images; 144 *microphone* ©Getty Images; 144 *vote sign* ©Photodisc/Getty Images; 145 *mitt and ball* ©Comstock/Getty Images; 155 *railroad train* ©Peter Kunasz/Shutterstock; 156 *mountains* ©Photodisc/Getty Images; 158 *prairie* ©Photodisc/Getty Images; 160 *prairie* ©Photodisc/Getty Images; 160 *cows* ©Photodisc/Getty Images; 162 *sneakers* ©Artville/Getty Images; 163 *box* ©Getty Images; 165 *colored pencils* ©Photodisc/Getty Images; 165 *clipboard* ©Artville/Getty Images; 166 *notepad* ©Artville/Getty Images; 166 *eraser* ©Photodisc/Getty Images; 166 *tape* ©Brand X Pictures/Stockbyte/Getty Images; 166 *pencil sharpener* ©Artville/Getty Images; 166 *ruler* ©Photodisc/Getty Images; 168 *pushpins* ©Artville/Getty Images; 169 *protractor* ©Artville/Getty Images; 170 *Stonehenge* ©Corbis; 171 *mason's brush* ©Squared Studios/Getty Images; 171 *mattock* ©Houghton Mifflin Harcourt; 174 *Stonehenge* ©Corbis; 176 *Stonehenge* ©Photodisc/Getty Images; 177 *Stonehenge* ©Corbis; 210-212 *rope* ©C Squared Studios/Photodisc/Getty

Images; 214 *rope* ©C Squared Studios/Photodisc/Getty Images; 216 *Oregon Trail* ©Brand X Pictures/Getty Images; 218-224 *napkin border* ©Photodisc/Getty Images; 226 *nine globes* ©Fotolia; 226 *horse chestnut* ©Martin Ruegner/Getty Images; 227 *five chestnuts* ©D. Hurst/Alamy; 227 *chestnut leaves* ©Creativ Studio Heinemann/Getty Images; 227 *five chestnuts* ©D. Hurst/Alamy; 227 *chestnut leaves* ©Creativ Studio Heinemann/Getty Images; 228 *Appalachian Mountains* ©Adam Jones/Digital Vision/Getty Images; 229 *erlenmeyer flask* ©Photodisc/Getty Images; 230 *golden autumn scenery with trees* ©Juliet photography/Shutterstock; 232 *woman on a fence* ©Jack Hollingsworth/Getty Images; 233 *five chestnuts* ©D. Hurst/Alamy; 233 *chestnut leaves* ©Creativ Studio Heinemann/Getty Images; 239 *dry corn cobs* ©Svetlana Foote/Shutterstock.

Copyright © by Houghton Mifflin Harcourt Publishing Company.